T0129140

THE UNMOCKABLE
MASTER

MELISSA SARGEANT-QUESTELLES

authorHOUSE®

AuthorHouse™
1663 Liberty Drive
Bloomington, IN 47403
www.authorhouse.com
Phone: 1 (800) 839-8640

Published by AuthorHouse   05/28/2015

ISBN: 978-1-5049-1184-9 (sc)
ISBN: 978-1-5049-1183-2 (e)

Library of Congress Control Number: 2015907607

Print information available on the last page.

KJV
Scripture quotations marked KJV are from the Holy Bible,
King James Version (Authorized Version). First published
in 1611. Quoted from the KJV Classic Reference Bible,
Copyright © 1983 by The <u>Zondervan</u> Corporation.

CONTENTS

ACKNOWLEDGEMENT

It is often said that 'no man is an island by himself.' At this point, I will like to express my deepest gratitude to a number of persons for making this book a reality, but first and foremost, let me say thanks to almighty God for guiding me in writing this book. A special thanks to Oral Roberts who did an excellent job in designing the cover. Sincere thanks to Sharva Maloney, Decima Hamilton and my husband, Kenroy Questelles for giving of their time so freely in proof reading my manuscript. Special thanks to my parents and siblings for their great words of encouragement during this challenging journey. If it wasn't for your support, this publication would have been impossible.

Who is a false prophet?

A false prophet can be recognized by the fact that he or she yields bad fruits, distrust, discord, confusion, wrangling, gossip, useless disputes and divisions within the church. (www.biblebell.org)

- ❖ A false prophet is one who falsely claims the gift of prophecy or divine inspiration, or who uses that gift for evil ends. (www.biblebell.org)

- ❖ False prophets whitewash evil. They dress up wickedness to make it presentable.

- ❖ False prophets work impressive miracles that deceive.

- ❖ False prophets teach rebellion against God in a subtle, skilful and well crafted manner.

- ❖ False prophets lift the scriptures out of context and adapt them to suit their many pitfalls.

- ❖ False prophets teach persons to crave worldly possessions by prophesying lies of blessings to their victims.

❖ False prophets have no respect for God; hence the reason for saying, "thus says the Lord," whenever they prophesy.

❖ False prophets put on a form of godliness to appear as an angel of light.

Fellow believers in Christ, Satan will do everything within his power to stop you from serving the Lord. We must seek the Lord with all our hearts to fully arm ourselves for the serious battle in which we are engage. Extremely strong faith in God's word, prayerfully studied and practically applied, will be our only shield from Satan's demonic power. He has already introduced counterfeits that are so deceptive, that if God's people do not maintain a very deep, living relationship with him, they will be deceived.

Let's take a look at Matthew chapter 24 verse 24. It says: 'For there shall arise false christs, and false prophets, and shall shew great signs and wonders; insomuch that, if it were possible, they shall deceive the very elect.'

The adversary usually creates an emotional excitement, a deep mingling of the truth with the lie that is skilfully, crafted and adapted to mislead. However, the Bible tells us in Matthew 7 verse 15-17: 'Beware of false prophets, which come to you in sheep's clothing, but inwardly they are ravening wolves. Ye shall know them by their fruits. Do men gather grapes of thorns, or figs of thistles? Even so every good tree bringeth forth good fruit; but a corrupt tree bringeth forth evil fruit.' Satan already has his agents set and aligned like powerful, sharp, pointed arrows to shoot at the Christians to darken and confuse their mind and root out the doctrine of salvation with their subtle fallacies, but 1 Corinthians 14 verse 33 tells us: 'For God is not the author of confusion, but of peace, as in all churches of the saints.' Are we truly prepared for the fiery trial which awaits us when the lying wonders of Satan shall be exhibited in its full force? How many more souls will be ensnared and taken? Though this is an intense battle to fight, we must always remember Isaiah 59 verse 19. 'When the enemy shall come in like a flood, the spirit of the Lord shall lift up a standard against him.' As children of God, we <u>must</u> go through some stormy times. We are going to be seriously wounded for the enemy is going to push us so hard, that it will cause our very faith in God to be shaken. Isaiah 43 verse 2 God says: 'When thou passeth through the waters, I will be with thee; and through the rivers, they shall not overflow thee: when thou walkest through the fire, thou shall not be burned; neither shall the flame kindle upon thee.'

They surrounded her like bees; they went out like a fire among thorns. In the name of the Lord she cut them off! She was pushed extremely hard; she was falling, but the good Lord firmly kept her from slipping!

CHAPTER 1

"So what you gonna do? What you gonna do? Am gonna roll my eye d-i-s-c-o. Step aside d-i-s-c-o, wine d-i-s-c-o and juke, juke, juke."

As the little grade two students behold Mrs. Guidance, they immediately stopped singing and fearfully ran upstairs. Inserting her key into the door, Mrs. Guidance could hear the sounds of 'pop pop' bursting upstairs.

As she entered the classroom, switched on the lights and put her books down; Kalifa a child in her class came running towards her claiming it was her birthday. She remembered four months ago, they sang happy birthday to her. Mrs. Guidance scolded her about the danger of telling lies. She looked as the child went into her red school bag, took some money and ran outside. Moments later, a crowd was seen around Kalifa. In her hands, she was carrying three large ice-creams. She was leading them towards the nearby court.

As Mrs. Guidance sat at her desk moments later, her right hand under her chin, she drifted off into thought. Even though she enjoyed her job from deep within, she felt something was amiss. Often times, she would reflect on the time she had accepted the Lord as her personal saviour at the tender age of twelve. It was an unforgettable experience. From the depth of her heart, she knew she would return to the Lord, but it was as though she was waiting for someone to encourage, hold and guide her. Adamma needed support. Occasionally, she would read her Bible and pray, but that wasn't enough. There was still a void within.

Mrs. Adamma Guidance was patiently biding to wait.

The newspapers she had purchased on Friday stared at her. Adamma Guidance was grateful for the weekends. She unfolded the papers and decided to read The Daily News.

"Taxi driver hospitalized after being doused with pepper, acid mixture and hot water. A man, who up to press time was visibly wincing from pain in his hospital bed, after suffering severe burns as a result of a substance being thrown on him, is crying for justice. The Daily News understands that at around twelve midnight on Saturday, while at home, it is alleged that an argument erupted between the man and his common-law wife, which resulted in him being burned with a substance on his face, chest and right arm."

"Boy, I wonder what that man did to that woman for her to do something like that. She was really soaking for him."

Adamma gazed long and hard into space trying to assess the unfortunate situation. "Lord, but he careless too, just after such a heated argument he lie down sleeping away."

As if on cue, she could then hear the loud talking of two men who stood at her gate.

"Boy, Raegan I do not understand some men, don't matter how much I try. Some times I just have to laugh."

"Boy, yeah true, some men just outright strange."

"Imagine Friday papers first thing I could see hit headlines, was police on hunt for Coco Village Woman. Boy, watch me, you will make a woman burn away your whole face?"

"It is not a matter of allowing her to do it, but the man was sleeping."

"Boy, even though I am sleeping no woman cannot 'monkey' around me. Up to press time I heard they cannot even locate her. I understand the man is still at the Tapion Hospital suffering from multiple burns to his body. Once you as a man 'liming' a woman, she has to respect you. You have to know when to draw the line with them or otherwise they tend to disrespect you. As the man you must put down the ground rules. When

you see them getting out off hand, you have to step up your game."

A loud laughter was heard.

"Devon, and how exactly is a man suppose to step up his game?"

Watching at her window, Adamma could see one of the guy's hand rested on her gate. *Not a bad question* she thought.

"Hmmmn, boy is it not surprising you asking a question like that."

"Man, just answer the question."

"Raegan, a man like you, I won't be surprised if a woman is calling the shots on you."

"Call shots on whom? You don't even know what you are saying."

"Man, I do not even feel like answering that question, the littlest child can answer that, but since we are partners, I will answer you. Seem like you need some coaching."

"Yeah, well coach me."

"Well, to put a woman on the right track when you find her getting out of control, all you have to do, is give her a 'black eye' every now and then and you would see how fast she respect you, as simple as that."

"Boy, Devon I am not in agreement with you when you start with that foolishness. If a woman and a man

cannot see eye to eye, the best thing to do is discontinue the relationship. A real man stands on his own feet and handle situation in a sensible manner."

A smile escaped Adamma's lips. She ducked from the window as the curtains blew.

"Raegan, boy you are not on the same level with me. You are not hitting her to cause damage to draw attention."

"Devon, you cannot treat a woman like a child. Watch, once a man start beating a woman, he will reach to a point where he cannot control himself. Why you think some women get their heads chopped off and all these kind of things? As the Bible is concerned, men are the head of the home, but how can a man lead his home when he isn't walking in accordance with the word of God?"

A defeated laugh came from Devon. He patted his friend's shoulder.

"Lord have mercy, Raegan is preaching for me. Boy, we are not at church. Man, I still feel as a man, you have to do something to help yourself. Some women behave like they want to put a rope around a man's neck and have them crawling behind them like some monkeys."

Adamma laughed aloud as she moved from the window. The guys had made her day.

As she settled down at her desk moments later to do her lesson plans, her telephone rang. It was her son Nathon calling from the United States of America. They chatted for an hour. As Adamma came off the phone, she thought about her son for a long moment. She hoped he was not getting caught up with any gang. Adamma sighed as she turned her attention back to her work. She knew it was going to be a long night with the mountain of work she had to cover.

CHAPTER 2

Mrs. Adamma Guidance waited for a van. She was grateful that her school was located next to the main road. The sun was shining in all its glory and splendour. Taking a piece of tissue from her bag, she wiped the beads of perspiration that were making their way down her forehead as she awaited the signal from the traffic warden. Moving her neck from side to side, she felt a sharp pain at the base of her neck. She sucked her teeth on seeing the appearance of cars, trucks and jeeps. Closing her eyes, she let out a yawn. She hoped Mrs. Aziyolata, a teacher at the St. Augustine Primary School did not meet her. Mrs. Aziyolata is never a busy woman. She would have long conversation with even the smallest child. Her slothful walking was what Mrs. Guidance dreaded. As Mrs. Guidance looked towards the school, she could see her walking along the corridor. On her arm she was carrying her workbag and a large green Vinlec bag that marked, '*I pledge to switch off unplug and save.*' Mrs. Guidance remembered the energy conservation slogan of the power company. Mrs. Aziyolata reached into her bag and gave a black plastic bag to a woman with whom she was speaking to. Mrs. Guidance remembered when Mrs. Aziyolata had brought a bag of stinging nettle bush to share among the staff, claiming it was good for high blood pressure and sugar. She wondered if it was some of those same bushes she gave the woman.

A bus appeared. Adamma sat next to a window. Someone gently tapped her shoulder. As she turned around, Sister Efia greeted her with a broad smile and threw both arms around her and kissed her right cheek. Sister Efia knew Mrs. Guidance since she was a little girl. They both had attended the same church when Mrs. Guidance had gotten baptized at age twelve. Mrs. Guidance knew Sister Efia was overjoyed to see her, after so many years of not attending church. They chatted excitedly about each other's well being and the latest progress that was taking place in their lives. She was then invited to a crusade at Nothing Hill. Sister Efia pleaded with her to attend the crusade because it would make a difference in her life. From deep within, Mrs. Guidance felt this was the support she needed. The gentle hand she was waiting on to help her along life's journey was now extended to her ever so softly.

CHAPTER 3

Gospel songs filled the air as people talked and moved to the back of the tent. The night was cold. A number of persons had their jackets thrown around them. Some sisters came to Sister Efia and greeted her while a few waved and continued their delegated task.

On the stage was a podium decorated in burgundy with a big, white cross to the front. The floor was also carpeted in burgundy. At the back, large thick burgundy drapes were hanging giving the surrounding a homey, comfortable feeling. To the front of the stage in a corner were a large piano and a drum set.

A group of female ushers was in a corner conversing. They were smartly dressed in black skirts, white shirts and maroon scarves. On their feet were black shoes. The men were in black pants, white shirts, maroon ties and black shoes.

Next to the tent was a mini version of the main tent. Inside, a group was holding hands and praying. Sister Efia informed her that they were people who were assigned to pray for the crusade.

Ten minutes later, a slim, fair man with lightly graying hair and a pair of glasses appeared on the stage.

"Goodnight everyone, what a great pleasure it is to be in the presence of the Lord. At this point, I would like to welcome everyone to our 'Victory in Christ Crusade.' Is there anyone who is visiting us for the very first time?" He asked, looking through the crowd.

"Mother, all of that too," muttered Mrs. Guidance standing to her feet.

"Wow, isn't she lovely, isn't she beautiful, could you just wave to us my sister?" The speaker commented while the crowd clapped.

Lord, like I come here tonight for you to make a fool of me.

"Welcome to our 'Victory in Christ Crusade' sister. I can tell you, you have chosen the right place to be tonight."

She smiled in agreement. An usher gave her a hugged and a book that captioned, 'Step to Christ.'

Two song service leaders led the congregation into a number of prayer songs. The preacher, Pastor Gaddiel was then introduced. There were loud clapping and shouts of amen. He was carrying a big stick painted in white.

"God is good," he chanted knocking the stick on the floor.

"All the time," the congregation roared with excitement.

A question box was brought on stage. The preacher was asked a number of questions pertaining to the Bible to which he answered clearing up misconceptions.

"Fellow believers, let us turn our Bibles to Isaiah 45 verses 2-3. My reader can you read that portion of scripture for me please?"

"I will go before thee, and make the crooked places straight: I will break in pieces the gates of brass, and cut in sunder the bars of iron: And I will give thee the treasures of darkness, and hidden riches of secret places, that thou mayest know that I, the Lord, which call thee by thy name, am the God of Israel."

Adamma could see a broad smile on the preacher's face.

"Saints of God, I am just in love with this particular scripture. You see there are some prayers that are uttered at midnight when we tossed and turned in our beds and it is impossible for us to sleep because our burdens are just too heavy and we are left with no other alternatives, but to go to God weeping. We are so deeply wounded and ripped that only God can heal our sorrows and calm our lurking fears. Our deep groaning is meant only for an infinite God, but according to Isaiah chapter 45 verses 2-3, *God will give you treasures of your darkness.* You had no idea that while you were sitting in the dark all alone with teary eyes, God was working behind the scenes. He was seeding something from deep within you that you have to give birth to. Can I preach the word of God tonight?"

Persons shouted and urged the preacher to continue.

"Fellow believers, God has to hide your treasure from the enemy, so what he does, he hid your treasures in very dark places so the enemy will not be able to destroy it. Sometimes not even you are aware of your hidden treasures until you start walking in your destiny."

Several persons stood and clapped as they received the word.

"Tonight I am here to defend my God! Some of us often say, if there is a God, then why does he allow suffering? God is all knowing, but sometimes he allows the attack of the enemy so that out of that same darkness, glory and honour can come to his name. It is out of our darkest moments in life that we often find our destiny. Our treasures are hidden in the very broken places of our lives. Ladies and gentlemen the Devil will go all out to destroy us, and above all, try to destroy our assigned task.

My people I am here to tell you tonight that you are precious in the sight of God, but the Devil is putting up an extremely strong fight to sift you. I know some of you here tonight feel as though you are in bondage, but let me tell you something, God is more than capable to loose all bondage. Whoever the father set free is free indeed. Some of you maybe saying, but pastor you don't understand the situation I am in. I may not know your situation tonight, but God knows it all. It is difficult for some of you to surrender your life because the Devil has got you so wrapped up and twisted in his dirty web, but I am saying to you tonight, push, push stepped out and come to Jesus tomorrow might just be too late."

He was pointing an index finger at the crowd.

"If you hear his voice harden not you heart. Please if you hear Jesus calling you forward tonight, step boldly to his throne of grace. With Jesus you have absolutely nothing to lose. And I will give thee the treasures of darkness and hidden riches of secret places, that thou mayest know that I am God. Come to Jesus tonight and he promised you in his words he will make your crooked ways straight."

As Adamma Guidance listen to the pastor's voice, she could feel a tug on her heart.

Girl, are you going up there to make a big fool of yourself? Everybody is going to be looking at you. You are simply just getting emotional. Behave yourself!

The preacher continued to urge people to give their life to Christ. Again, she felt that strong tugged on her heart. It was so strong that it was impossible to resist. Mrs. Guidance stepped forward. It was as though she made an opening. Within a short space of time, many were at the pulpit. Some persons were crying. The song, 'Pass me not o gentle saviour' was sung twice. The persons at the pulpit, were given cards to write their names, contact number and anything thing they need special prayer for. Moments later, as Adamma Guidance walked away, Sister Efia was right beside her embracing her and telling her how proud she was. Sister Efia's face was awashed with tears. Not wanting to get emotional, Mrs. Guidance looked away. Hand in hand they walked towards the blue bus that was assigned to take home people from the crusade. Mrs. Adamma Guidance felt her soul was at peace.

CHAPTER 4

"May the grace of our Lord and Saviour Jesus Christ the love of God and the fellowship of the Holy Spirit be with us all now and forever more amen."
You are going to take your time and repeat the grace Mrs. Guidance said to her students.

Moments later, after clearing away her desk and walking up the steps and making her entrance into the main road, her mind drifted to the crusade; no way was she going to miss out. Adamma Guidance was desperate to hear the word of God.

The service followed the same order. As the Evangelist Gaddiel came on, a smile crossed her face.

"Welcome to the 'Victory in Christ Crusade.' Father as we are about to go through your words, inspired us, opened our minds and hearts in Jesus name amen. Let me just read to you briefly the three angels message from Revelation chapter 14 verse 6-12 because of time, I would be going quickly so please pay attention. And I saw another angel fly in the midst of heaven, having the everlasting gospel to preach unto them that dwell on the earth and to every nation, and kindred and tongue, and people. And this is what the angel said in a loud voice, fear God, and give glory to him; for the hour of his judgment is come: and worship him that made heaven, and earth, and the sea, and the fountains of waters. And here is what the second angel said, Babylon is fallen, is fallen, that great city, because she made all nation drink of the wine of the wrath of her fornication. And the third angel followed them, saying with a loud voice, if any man worship the beast and his image, and receive his mark in his forehead, or in his hand, the same shall drink of the wrath of God, which is poured out without mixture into the cup of his indignation; and he shall be tormented with fire and brimstone in the presence of the holy angels, and in the presence of the lamb. And the smoke of their torment ascendeth up forever and ever: and they have no rest day or night, who worships the beast and his image, and whosoever receiveth the mark of his name. Here is the patience of the saints: here are they that keep the commandments of God, and the faith of Jesus.

Let us analyze the text closely. *It says fear God and give him glory*. In examining this scripture, one can clearly say that this is a strong message coming from heaven. In order for such message to come from heaven it means that something went terrible wrong somewhere. Turn your Bibles with me to Revelation chapter 12 verses 7-8 and the Bible says: And there was war in heaven: Michael and his angels fought against the dragon; and the dragon fought and his angels, and prevailed not; neither was their place found anymore in heaven. Now let us go to Revelation chapter 12:9: And the great dragon was cast out, that old serpent, called the Devil, and Satan that deceiveth the whole world: he was cast out into the earth, and his angels were cast out with him. The Prophet Isaiah asked the Devil a question and he refused to answer. Let us take a look at Isaiah chapter 14 verse 12: How art thou fallen from heaven? As we say in Hairouna Island, ah wey yo ah do down ya? The Devil did not answer and Isaiah continues, for thou hast said in thine heart, I will exalt my throne above the stars of God.

Now remember in heaven the Devil caused division. So if he is cast out into the earth, what do you think will happen here? There will be division as well. It will be Michael and his angels and the dragon and his angels. Lucifer came from within God's government. That is why his accusations were so believable. Let us go to Ezekiel chapter 28:15, 17: Thine heart was lifted up because of thy beauty, thou hast corrupted thy wisdom by reason of brightness. Thou was perfect in thy ways from the day that thou was created, till iniquity was found in thee. Lucifer has a great desire to take God's position and so, he is competing strongly with God for lasting supremacy.

Fellow believers in Christ, the enemy is going to do all things that are possible to stop you from serving the Lord, but if you hear the voice of Jesus calling you, harden not your heart."

Once again, the pastor was making another altar call for people to surrender their lives to Jesus. A number of persons were already at the front.

"Those of you, who were here last night, could you please come forward."

What is the matter with this man? I have already dedicated my life to God last night and now he calling me back. Girl, girl get a grip of yourself and stop that rebellious attitude.

Mrs. Adamma Guidance joined the others. The evangelist asked them to go to the back of the tent.

My world, what is this?

Another pastor was there encouraging them to go with Jesus all the way by getting baptized.

But I thought I rededicated my life by going up at the pulpit, now they talking about baptism. Lord, you could tell me what I really get myself into. Trouble makes the 'monkey' eat pepper. Stop, stop, stop that behaviour girl!

As she walked from beneath the tent with Sister Efia's hand holding hers, they boarded the awaiting blue bus along with many others. As the bus journeyed onward, Mrs. Adamma Guidance was deep in thought. She was extremely troubled.

Half an hour later, as she arrived home and changed her clothes, Adamma was seriously wrestling with herself. It was an unhappy battle. She felt as though she had no peace within. The ringing of the telephone interfered with her thought.

"Hello."

It was Sister Efia.

"Adamma, you have a serious decision to make, but don't let Satan hinder you. Have you made up your mind to get baptize?"

"I am thinking about it, but do I have to do it right now can't I wait until I am fully ready?"

"Adamma, you are supposed to put God first. I know your decision is going to be tough because the enemy wants you badly, he knows what you are capable of doing."

"I know, I know all of that, but it is just that I thought I could have gone to the pulpit and accept Jesus back into my life. I have never known I have to go through all this baptism again."

She could hear a small chuckle.

"What is so funny?"

"I am just listening at how Satan is battling with you. He is wrestling with you, but don't let him win. What if you die Adamma where would you spend eternity?"

"Please pray for me."

"I am going to do exactly that. I will call my husband and we will pray for you."

As she hung up the phone, Sister Efia's words wore heavy on her mind.

Why this woman had to bring in death into this thing boy?

CHAPTER 5

With heavy beads of perspiration running down her forehead, she forced with all her might to get over the steep hill, but all her efforts were futile. Realizing time was closing in; Adamma Guidance stuck a piece of iron rod into the concrete. As she stepped on it, it gave way. Feeling defeated, she stared helplessly at the steep stretch of hill. Within her heart she knew many others have traveled that road. How they made it, could have only been a miracle. A lump rose in her throat. Her tears were falling. Suddenly, she felt cold.

Her eyes fluttered open and she closed the bedroom window. Adamma realized it was a dream. It was as though she was climbing the hill in reality. She was tired. Opening her right hand, she stretched it back as far as she could, until it pained. It reminded her of the steep hill. Adamma pondered on the meaning. She made a few phone calls to her relatives, but no one knew what her dream meant. Adamma Guidance knew this will be a dream she would remember for a long, long time.

CHAPTER 6

In the blood from the cross
I have been washed from sin;
But to be from dross....

Standing on Nothing Hill Beach in a long, grey, slightly faded gown with many others, Mrs. Adamma Guidance listened to the melodious singing of those who were witnessing their baptism. The water was reaching Pastor Gaddiel at his chest. There was a long line of persons to be baptized. As she looked over to the nearby grape trees, Sister Efia smiled and gave her the thumbs up. A sudden wind caused Sister Efia to hold her white hat. Adamma faced what was taking place. She was fighting a hard battle from deep within. It was so powerful, that Adamma turned her head to look at the others. She wondered if they were going through the same thing as well. Nevertheless, she stood her ground until she was next. The singing had stopped as she stepped into the water. The pastor instructed her to hold his right hand with both hands as he lifted up his left hand.

"This morning Adamma Guidance has decided to go all the way with Jesus into the watery grave of baptism. 2 Corinthians 5:17: says: Therefore if any man be in Christ, he is a new creature: old things are passed away; behold, all things are new."

She was dipped into the water. As she made her way out, she saw the woman who was behind her stepping into the water.

Adamma slowly walked to the nearby changing room. As she pushed open the door of one of the rooms, the slim, narrow feature woman with short hair that was right behind her, flashed a bright smile which she gingerly returned.

"Go inside. I'll be the watchwoman. Anybody come, they will have to pass through me."

Adamma Guidance laughed loudly. She knew instantly, she had found a friend. As she slipped into the room, she realized the woman was right; there was no bolt. After changing her clothes and slipping out, she allowed the woman to change.

They walked and chatted as they headed towards the tent to await the hands of fellowship. She listened attentively as her friend told her how excited she was that she gave her life to Christ. She spoke about a rough life she had and how she almost committed suicide. Adamma eyed her closely, as she wondered what rough life this young woman could have had. She estimated her age to be eighteen.

"One thing though, we forget to introduce ourselves. My name is Adamma," she laughed.

"I am Parisa."

They continued chatting as though they had no cares in the world. Suddenly, Parisa looked at her a bit uncomfortably.

"I know they like to talk about testimonies from new converts, but trust me I don't like that part. I really cannot handle that."

"It's not everyone who likes to open up to give a testimony. Some persons are private and we have to respect that."

"They could just do the hands of fellowship encourage us to be strong in the Lord and let us go home." Adamma nodded in agreement.

"Oh I forget my manners. I was so taken up with you. This is the lady whom I lived with, her name is Haala Snow." She pointed to a dark, round face woman that was sitting directly behind.

"Hi, it is nice meeting you," the woman replied, smiling broadly.

As she continued to talk with her friend, she found out they were living within close proximity and they would be attending the same church.

One hour later, Pastor Gaddiel congratulated the new converts. They listened as he reported that there was not much time to do testimonies. Parisa and Adamma smiled as relief flooded them. The pastor informed the congregation that there would be no service that afternoon because of the baptism.

"Even though we are pressed for time, I could squeeze in at least one response from one of our new converts. I am certain she has something to say."

Unexpectedly, a mike was thrust into Mrs. Guidance's hand. Her heart was racing dramatically.

Lord, if you really know better pastor, you will do better. Facing the congregation she spoke.

"Today, I am happy that I gave my life to the Lord before it was too late. If I am to die this moment, I know exactly where I will spend eternity."

She could hear loud amen from the congregation. The new converts were then called to the front. Members from the congregation shook their hands welcoming them into the faith. They were encouraged to walk with Christ and were strongly warned that the Christian pathway could be difficult at times.

As Adamma walked from the tent, she and Parisa were busy talking. Meanwhile the woman Parisa lived with followed and joined in the conversation intermittently. Adamma wasted no time in introducing them to Sister Efia.

She knew she had made the right decision. Adamma Guidance heart was at peace that void she was feeling previously, no longer haunted her.

CHAPTER 7

Her newly found friends in Christ were calling her. Briskly, stepping outside she locked the door. Walking down the steps was a challenge. She had to be fending off her troublesome dog Frisky whose aim was to jump right on her white skirt. It was a great struggle to reach the gate. The others, especially Haala's son, Adonnas laughed at the scenario. As Adamma reached at the gate, the dog stood on its hind legs and projected its' paws. Gently, she patted the animal on its forehead as she proceeded through the gate. As usual, she felt its' wet tongue licking her fingers. She greeted her friends with a warm hug. They took a bus to the Higher Calling Church.

They occupied seats at the front. Adamma was missing Sister Efia who worshipped at a branch that was closer to her home. As the congregation blended their voices together, Adamma meditated upon the words.

"*O day of rest and gladness, O day of joy and light, O balm of care and sadness.*"

She was in the right place. *What joy it is to be in the holy presence of the Lord,* she thought. One hour later, as the congregation was divided into their respective classes to do the lesson study; a tall slightly graying man wearing a glasses stood and spoke.

"For the new converts, I am Brother Padon one of your class teachers."

A smile crossed Adamma's face as she nodded.

He adjusted his glasses and continued.

"Today, our lesson study is captioned, '*discipling through metaphor.*' *Let us repeat the memory verse. Jesus spoke all these things to the crowd in parables; he did not say anything to them without using a parable so was fulfilled what was spoken through the prophet: I will open my mouth in parables; I will utter things hidden since the creation of the world." (Matthew 13:34, 35 NIV)* They chanted in unison.

"Why Jesus used parables?" he asked.

"To avoid risking his death before time, if Jesus did not use parables he would have called peoples' names and this would have caused serious confrontation.

Therefore he had to exercise wisdom," replied Sister Adamma.

"Wonderful, well said," agreed the teacher. A few of the others shook their heads in agreement.

"Using a literary device (a parable), Nathan accomplishes something that otherwise might have caused his death when he went to speak to King David. Let us pick up on the story in 2 Samuel chapter 12. Nathan told the king a parable about a rich man and a poor man. When King David heard how the rich man dealt wickedly with the poor man, he was furious at him and strongly believed the rich man should be put to death, only to realize that the rich man was him. David killed Uriah the Hittite with the sword, and took his wife. By using a parable, Nathan was able to soften the king's heart and finally got to the core of the matter."

Together they looked at a number of parables in the Bible that Jesus spoke and examined them which created an exciting lesson discussion.

At twelve thirty the service was dismissed, after greeting a number of the members, Mrs. Guidance and her three friends took a bus and headed home. They were so overjoyed with their relationship with God, they held hands and prayed asking him to continue granting them mercy so they could continue to serve him. Mrs. Guidance smiled, as she inserted the key into the door.

She was going to cherish her relationship with God and nothing was going to come between them. Absolutely nothing!

CHAPTER 8

As she took a green jacket from the pink, broad, wash pan and hung it on the line and was about to walk up the steps, Adamma Guidance saw Parisa, Haala and her son Adonnas standing at her gate smiling. She immediately tied the dog and smiled all the way to unlock the gate. They were carrying their Bibles and song books. A jolt of excitement rushed through her. Adamma was drinking from the fountain of everlasting peace. Accepting the Lord had brought such joy. Her heart was bursting with a happiness she could hardly contain.

"Wow, this is such a wonderful surprise."

"Adamma, we have to visit you. We are sisters in Christ and we have to take care of each other."

She could hear the excitement in the older woman's voice. As she opened the house, she ushered them inside. Sitting on the couch, she couldn't help, but smiled happily at them. It was as though they knew each other for years. After chatting excitedly about a number of different things, Haala decided they must accomplish what they came for. The older woman set the pace.

"Parisa, you will open in a word of pray."

"Dear kind and heavenly Father as we about to fellowship here this afternoon, may you just lead out and have your way. May our pray be acceptable in thy sight o Lord and our redeemer for Christ sake amen."

Their fellowship session began in honest as they sang lustily three hundred and seventeen.

King of my life, I crown thee now
Thine shall the glory be;
Lest I forget thy thorn-crowned brow....

A few hours later, she walked her friends to the gate and bid them farewell. Walking under the house, Adamma untied the dog that played wildly. Frisky licked her feet, hands and consistently jumped on her. Having an excellent day, Mrs. Guidance took the dog's face into her hands and stared at it smiling for a long, long time.

CHAPTER 9

The vendors that were stationed at the entrance of the St. Agustine School were busy every morning. Students were busy flocking their trays. On few occasions, one could hear Miss Odeda speaking to a number of students not to push against the tray, because they were squeezing the life out of her. The sounds of coins could be heard as the vendors dug into their plastic bags to deposit money and make change.

As she walked along the corridor, Mrs. Adamma Guidance could see the blue, red, green and yellow tongues of a number of children.

As the bell rang, Mrs. Guidance took prayers with her children and began preparing them for class.

"Please, if you listen to me you will do the correct thing. I said all the boys will line up along side each other over here and all the girls will do the same over there. You will then face each other. The boys will call the masculine gender and the girls will chant the feminine gender. Is that clear?

"Yes Mrs. Guidance," they responded.

A few hours later, as the bell rang she dismissed her class; Mrs. Guidance took a bus and went home.

One hour later, her phone rang. It was Sister Haala calling to have fellowship. Half an hour became an hour. The women had spent quality time glorifying God. The more time they spent with God, it was the more they want to be in his presence. Mrs. Guidance had never experienced anything so wonderful. As she hung up the phone; her heart was bursting with love. Sitting in her chair, she instinctively called her aunt and went directly into pray. It took a long time for her aunt to respond she almost thought she had hung up.

"Adamma, it is the Lord sent you to call me. I was feeling so depressed. I just felt like throwing in the towel. The tears kept bathing me. A moment later, I heard my phone ringing and it was you."
She listened as her aunt unfolded her problem to her and was glad her call brought comfort.

Lying on the couch on her back, Adamma spoke.

"God, I am here, use me anytime you want to. Anytime, anywhere, anything for you God, anything!" she said sincerely from the depth of her heart.

CHAPTER 10

It was as though Haala and Adamma had a silent agreement. As she came from school, Haala would gave her time to settle down, do her chores then call her to praise and glorify God. This went on for more than three years. A well knitted, strong, friendship was formed. The women confided in each other as they encouraged each other on their Christian pathway. Anytime a problem arose they knew they could speak to each other and pray about the matter. At church, people recognized they were destined to serve God and were willing to play an active part in his temple. When it was time to do song service both women would do it, sang special songs and worked along. One church member had openly said they were like two shinning stars. Parisa was the bridge in bringing them together. She was mostly around the younger women.

Her phone rang. It was Haala. She sensed something was troubling her.

"Ada, I want you to pray for Parisa. It is just like she wants to go back into her old ways and I don't like it. There isn't anything in this world for her. Instead she moved forward in Christ; I am seeing some ungodly action in her. Ad let us be serious with our walk with

Christ. Let our goal be to make it into heaven to live with our eternal Father. Sister, there isn't anything in this world for us to look back for. If I am doing something wrong, don't be afraid to correct me and if you are doing something wrong, I won't be afraid to correct you. We have to make it into heaven!"

Adamma listened attentively. She could hear great compassion and sincerity in Haala's voice.

"Yes Sister Haala our main goal is to make it into heaven and we will help each other along that path."

She listened as Haala called the younger woman. As she came on the phone, Adamma prayed asking God to remove the shackles the enemy has placed on her. As Haala came back on the phone, she later informed Adamma it was quite some time since she was thinking of sending Parisa overseas to seek a job. She confided it was rough and Parisa needed to start helping herself. Two hours later, the women said goodbye. Adamma prayed to God to grant her friends what was best.

"Let your will be done for them Lord, your will," she said as sleep took over.

CHAPTER 11

Monday the 19th of March, 1995 was a day Mrs. Adamma Guidance will never forget. It was already four o' clock in the morning. She knew Parisa and Haala would be at the airport. It was the day Parisa was traveling to Canada to seek a better life. Even though Adamma was sad; she was grateful she had gotten the opportunity to say a proper goodbye. Sister Haala and Adamma were able to encourage and pray with Parisa. Parisa hugged Adamma as she was about to leave her home, and vowed never to forget her. As she walked down the steps from Adamma's home, she turned and smiled.

"Even though I will not be here, you and Haala still have each other," she said assuringly.

She looked as they headed towards the gate. Mrs. Guidance thought for a while, *just as Parisa entered into my life quickly she was leaving in that same manner.*

"If you don't try, you will never be able to do anything," Mrs. Guidance warned a few of her students who were reluctant in drawing the digestive system, claiming it was too difficult. As she retraced the small intestine, she heard Tyreke calling.

"Mrs. Guidance."

"Yes."

"Look Kachada, Justin and Lael eating bread and chicken and they threw the bones under the desk."

"Boy, you see somebody eating any bread and chicken," shouted an aggressive Justin with an offending frown.

As she walked towards the three boys, she caught a glimpse of Justin's thumb smeared with ketchup.

"I thought I heard you said you were not eating."

Justin remained silent with down cast eyes.

"The three of you come."

Reluctantly, they walked to her desk. Justin's shirt was out of his pants as he stood bare feet.

"How many times I have to tell you to put your shirt into your pants and leave your shoes on your feet? Are you a vagrant?"

"No miss."

Moments later, after disciplining the boys, she looked at her time. As she closed her cupboard, the bell rang.

Mrs. Guidance couldn't believe her bad luck as she waited at the side of the road for a bus. Her right shoe had unstuck. Luckily, she had walked with a pair of flats. Looking at her watch, it was eight minutes past three. If she gets a bus quick she would be able to go straight into Queenstown and browse for a shoe.

Twenty minutes later, Mrs. Guidance was going through the stores trying on shoes and putting them back on the shelves. As she exited the Bucadi Store, she walked up a long flight of steps that lead to a boutique. A woman was sitting on a chair. The lady rose and greeted her with a smile.

"How can I help you?" She asked politely.

"Good afternoon," she said as she gazed along the glass case that was showcasing a wide variety of shoes. "I am looking for a shoe to wear to school," she informed the lady.

She looked as the lady went around the glass case and pointed out a number of shoes. A bronze, high heel had caught her attention which she later purchased. The attendant's demeanor encouraged Mrs. Guidance to have a conversation. She later learnt they were in the same faith. As she was about to leave, the lady ever so gentle held her hand and prayed. Suddenly, the woman began to make revelations.

"Thus saith the Lord, Adamma you are a pleasant person. You are on a spiritual height. You have gotten a dream, but no one could have interpreted it. Adamma what the Lord was saying to you then, you are chosen to go on in the last days."

She felt the woman gentle squeezing her hands and releasing it. Tears were running down her cheeks. Adamma Guidance knew the woman was truly a woman of God.

"Thank you so much," she said, feeling embarrassed that she had made a fool of herself.

As she exited the boutique, her thought was on the woman. The dream she had climbing the steep hill came to memory and more tears flowed. Softly, she spoke a few words to God.

"Father, I am so happy that you found me pleasant."

It was one of the best days of her life.

CHAPTER 12

The class teacher, Mr. Padon could be seen adjusting his glasses. With his quarterly in his hand, he looked at the class.

"For our lesson study today, we are going to be looking at the Prophet Amos. Our lesson study is captioned seek the Lord and live. Let us repeat the memory verse."

"Seek good and not evil, that you may live; and thus may the Lord God of hosts be with you, just as you have said!" (Amos 5:14, NASB)

"This week, as we continue to study the book of the Prophet Amos chapter 5:verses 1-15, we will see the Lord is pleading with the people to turn away from their sins and return unto him, the only true source of life. For this reason the Prophet Amos composed a lament to mourn the coming death of Israel."

One of the class members was raising her hand.

"One vital point we must always remember is that when we sin against God, we wrongeth our own souls and love death. This is something we must always keep in our heads."

A number of persons were nodding in agreement.

"Based on what our sister said, do you think Israel was thinking anywhere along that line?" asked the teacher.

"If they were thinking about God in the first place, how did they manage to reach so deep into sin? It simple tells us their hearts were far from God. Why do you think the Bible urges us to bind the word of God on our hands and around our necks? So we could keep God's words near," replied Sister Duncanise.

With his head bowed in the quarterly, he continued, "according to Isaiah 5:20: it says here, woe unto them, that call evil good, and good evil; that put darkness for light, and light for darkness; that put bitter for sweet, and sweet for bitter. One thing we have to remember here, is that Satan will work with all his deceptive power to influence the heart and becloud the understanding, to make evil appear good, and good evil."

Brother Padon called Sister King, "Permit me to share a point with the class."

"Go ahead sis."

"We know that Amos was a true prophet sent by God, but if we look at Amos 7:10-14 in a nut shell one could gather the people were fed up with Amos. If we look at verses twelve to thirteen, it says also Amaziah said unto Amos, o thou seer, go, flee thee away into the land of Judah, and there eat bread, and prophesy there: but prophesy not again any more at Bethel: for it is the King's chapel, and it is the King's court. Sometimes people don't want to hear the truth. They get tired and angry over it, but if you could give them sweet prophecy they will gravitate towards it."

"I like that point sister, but one thing we must remember and keep in mind even though long ago when the Lord sent harsh message through his prophets is because behind almost all the warnings is the call of redemption."

Moments later, the superintendent rang the bell causing the interesting lesson study to be dismissed. Two and a half hours later, the church service was dismissed. As the congregation made their exit, there were a number of persons hugging and shaking hands. It was a great pleasure to fellowship with each other. It was a day they looked forward to.

"Ada I was calling you yesterday, where were you? Your phone kept on ringing the whole time and I was so worried."

"Haala, I had to go straight into town to buy a shoe. My right shoe unstuck right in the road. It was a lucky thing I had my flats."

As they waited for a bus to go home, Haala spoke.

"Ada, one of my cousins along with her daughter will be coming from Trinity Island. They will be staying with us."

"Well nobody happy as you, you will have all the company in the world. You might not even remember to call me for us to pray," teased Adamma.

"Girl, nothing is going to come between my God and I."

"How old is your cousin's daughter?"

"She is about two."

Adamma told her about the lady whom she met when she went to purchase her shoes. Her friend was also in strong agreement that the woman was definitely a woman of God.

After exiting the bus, Haala quickly walked to catch up with her son who was always a few steps ahead of her.

CHAPTER 13

"Father as we about to begin our first staff meeting for the term may you be in the midst oh great God helping us to make the correct decisions for our students. May you bless us all as teachers in Jesus' name amen."

Mrs. Guidance hoped the meeting didn't take long. Her eyes quickly scanned the agenda. *Welcome, reading of minutes/correction/amendment/adoption, matters arising, correspondence, principal's report, teachers' responses, any other business and adjournment.*

"Teachers I must say welcome to another school term, without you, as the head I wouldn't be able to function. You are like my backbone. As we about to make decisions for our school and children please feel free to share your opinions. At this point, I will call on Mr. John to read the minutes."

"Mrs. Pear I think we should leave out the reading of the minutes. All our teachers could read so therefore I will go down the different sub headings and let teachers make corrections and amendments as they see fit."

"Last school term Mrs. Guidance would have attended a reading and comprehension workshop. I will give her an opportunity to share with us."

"As teachers we were advised to always introduce our lessons in an interesting manner to get our students' attention. It was observed that some teachers fell short in that area. The use of differentiating teaching was encouraged. We were cautioned that no two students are alike. Therefore, we must continue to tailor our lesson to meet the needs of our students."

She then highlighted and demonstrated the different strategies teachers could use to meet the needs of their students.

At four the meeting was over.

As Mrs. Aziyolata and Mrs. Guidance boarded a bus, she heard her cell phone ringing.

"Hello."

"Ada it's me. Where are you?"

"I'm in a bus going home."

"Girl, I need your help. I need a dress for church. I want something that fits nice," said Haala.

"Okay. Where do I meet you?"

"I am upstairs the Florist looking around."

"Okay cool. We'd link up."

Twenty minutes later, as she made her way upstairs the Florist, Haala was coming down the steps.

"Girl, I haven't seen anything sensible upstairs the Florist. All those people have is a whole heap of back-out clothes. Like they forget Christians live in the world too!"

"Let's get on the move."

They walked from store to store with Haala trying on clothes that were not to her satisfaction. Their shopping looked as though it was going to be a big disappointment and time was closing in on them.

"Adamma what about the woman you told me about who has the boutique, the one who made the revelations."

"Girl, you right. She has a lot of stuff."

As Haala and Adamma entered the boutique, the lady was attending a customer who was trying on a hat. A few minutes later, as the customer walked out, Adamma introduced her friend. A floral, nice looking, blue and white dress was selected. As Haala disappeared into the changing room, Adamma and her sister in faith chatted comfortably about school among other things.

"Ada" called Haala a few minutes later.

As she opened the door to the dressing room, a broad smile was on Haala's face. The dress was an ideal fit. It was conservative yet fashionable. Haala paid the one hundred and thirty five dollars and joined the conversation. As they were about to leave, Sister Cairoshell informed them about the prayer meeting she had on a Monday and Wednesday at ten o' clock. They were led to a section that revealed a prayer room. Haala joyfully accepted the invitation. As they were about to leave, Sister Cairoshell offered to pray with them. They joined hands as she asked God for traveling mercies and continued guidance over their lives. She then later revealed that the Lord said their common goal is to make it into heaven. They were also informed that there was going to be a great fire in Queenstown and a lot of persons were going to commit suicide like never before. Walking out the prayer room moments later, Haala and Adamma spoke excitedly. They were especially amazed when Sister Cairoshell revealed their common goal. Their hearts were lifted heaven ward.

CHAPTER 14

"Good morning Mrs. Guidance."

"Good morning Head Teacher."

"Mrs. Guidance my heart is burden. It is heavy this morning. Imagine yesterday, when some of your students were going home, they were seen on Kent's plum tree swinging their lives away. Mrs. Guidance those children could have fallen into the river or even broke their necks. Please permit me a few minutes of your lesson to speak to them."

"Good morning grade five."

"Good morning Head Teacher," they said as they stood.

"Please take your seats. Grade five, I want you to listen carefully. I understand some of you right in this class were swinging on Kent's plum tree. You are not wild animals you are little children and I expect you to conduct yourselves as such. What if you had broken your necks? I want no more report of such behaviour. Do you understand me?"

Mickey who was ever ready for the head teacher to leave and was not paying close attention replied loudly, "thank you miss and same to you."

"You know your place! I don't do these things, talking about thank you miss and same to you. Kiel, Lenora, Kenox, Loya, Venetta and Vishna come with me please. Thank you Mrs. Guidance just let me have a private word with these students."

"Sure Mrs. Pear." She looked as the head teacher marched out the classroom, the children strolling behind.

Folding her hands, Mrs. Guidance stared at the students.

"Mickey it pays to listen. You must learn to listen first and then speak after. You are so programmed to say thank you miss and same to you, that you are using it for anything your mind tells you. You have to be careful. Do you understand me?"

"Yes miss," he muttered playing with an exercise book while the others laughed.

As she took the last bit of her tuna sandwich, she picked up the ringing phone. "Hello."

"Hello Ada, I am sorry I couldn't call you before after prayer meeting. I felt so tired."

"It is okay. I understand. How was it though?" Adamma anxiously asked.

"It was great! There were so many people, and girl I actually felt the presence of the Holy Spirit in that place."

"Girl, you are making me feel left out and you know how I like to worship God."

"Well today we glorified God with the singing of songs. While we were singing, Ada in my heart, I was wishing for them to sing, 'Pass me not o gentle saviour.' I didn't want to ask them to sing it because it was my first time going and you know I was a bit shy. Soon after, we did that song. Girl the Holy Spirit was at work in that place. We prayed a lot and when it was Sister Cairoshell's turn, she made a lot of revelations today based on what the Holy Spirit revealed. Sister Cairoshell said, the Lord said, I will be a very strong pillar to the prayer meeting. Ada you know we always pray together and you know how much we love God, but she can't just know that. I am giving God my all and the woman revealed that."

"She'd know because she is filled with the Holy Spirit."

"She said the Lord said we must visit the hospital twice per month and pray with the sick."

"Well Haala you have your work cut out for you."

"Ada I don't mind, once it is for the Lord, I have no problem."
"That is true Haala once God wants his children to do something, we must be obedient."

"The Lord also revealed to her, it is time for the members of the prayer meeting to wear white."

"Do you have white clothes Haala?"

She could hear some sniffling.

"What happen?"

"Ada, is when I reflect on the goodness of God, the tears flow at times. When I came home, the first thing I did was search to see if I had anything white. I was saying too, I can't afford to buy any clothes again because remember it is only my husband working and my son is going to school. Ada, I opened the clothes cupboard and when I almost reached to the bottom, I got a nice, white skirt that my sister had given me a long time. I will wear it with a white top I have."

"God doesn't give a man more than he could bear. I am so sorry I couldn't be there too. It is a pity I have to teach."

"It is the same thing I said Ad. I wish you were there. You are just like a sister to me and such a wonderful close friend. The prayer meeting would have helped you even more on your Christian pathway."

As the two friends hang up the phone moments later, Adamma sat in a chair in her kitchen and thought about all that she was missing.

As she thought more of the situation, Adamma knew God knows exactly what he is doing he would make a way when there seems to be no way. No good things will he withhold from them that walk upright.

CHAPTER 15

Every Mondays and Wednesdays Haala would update Adamma on what was taking place at the prayer meetings. On few occasions she was told there were no revelations which made her disappointed. Adamma liked hearing from the Lord. Haala had been informed that Sister Cairoshell only reveals things when the Holy Spirit impress upon her heart to speak. As her phone rang, she picked up the receiver smiling.

"Hello."

Not in the mood for pleasantries Haala cut to the chase.

"Ad you know Sister Cairoshell revealed that many attempts were made to take my life and one recently, but she said the Lord said do not be afraid. My life is in his hands. Ad, I know Sister Cairoshell is speaking the truth because long before I got baptized, a man had tried to kill me."

"But Haala she said one recently as well, why will someone wants to kill you? You don't trouble anybody."

"Ad I am not even going to worry and fret because the Lord already said, my life is in his hands."

"That's true."

"Sister Cairoshell said the Lord said many more persons will be coming into the prayer meeting and she will have to get a bigger place. She also revealed the Lord is going to bring down Pastor Fairmont because he no longer walks in the light. Girl she also revealed a lot of women have their eyes on my husband, but the Lord said he has protected him. He has set a special mark upon him. Ada and to be honest with you, that is so true. Well you know Afaratanisa and her children usually come at my home and girl the last time she came by me, I wasn't please at all with her dressing. If you see the top she had on, a tight, tight top with two of the buttons opened and you could see all her cleavage, and she sat down right in front the door where my husband and all the other men were working. I had to call her aside and tell her, once she is coming at my home, she has to dress properly! Ada, those people are nothing but evil spirits and every time they come around I am always picking up on them. Sister Cairoshell said I have the discernment of spirit as well."

"God knows what he is doing. He knows if your marriage is affected so will your prayer life."

"True, true Ada I like how you reasoned things. One more thing I had forgotten to tell you girl, we were praying today in circles and Ada when it was my turn to pray, girl a power came down on me. My prayer was so powerful. I have never prayed so. I knew the words came from the Holy Spirit."

"It is so good when we can glorify God and gave him our all."

"Oh I just remember one more thing; she said the Lord said soon my husband and I are going to be blessed with a large lump sum of money and anything I put my hands to do, I will be successful at it."

"To God be the glory, Haala that has to be from God. The last time I came at your home and we were in the bedroom talking, I looked into the roof and I saw a lot of holes and girl in my mind, I was saying God, you really need to bless Haala, look at how she gives you her all. Girl I am so surprised to hear you telling me this now."

"Yes we really do need a financial blessing, and remember God promised he will provide for his own."

One hour later, Adamma took a warm bath and talked to God about the wonderful things he was about to do in her friend's life. She later telephoned her son Nathon and let him know how much his mom was missing him. She then drifted off to sleep peacefully.

CHAPTER 16

The atmosphere was buzzing with the number of persons who have committed suicide. Never in the history of Hairouna Island had so many persons taken their own lives. One woman commented it was as though suicide was in fashion. Teachers were seen and heard in their own corners talking about the suicide victims. Adamma Guidance was reading the papers and following closely to what was taking place. She remembered Sister Cairoshell had prophesied that the Lord said many persons were going to commit suicide. Adamma couldn't wait to reach home; Haala would be waiting on her. Half an hour later, she dismissed her students and packed away her books.

Her fixed line was ringing, as she searched in her bag for the key. Adamma opened the door, threw her bag on the chair and proceeded straight to the phone. As she was about to pick it up, it stopped then started ringing again. The two friends chatted for an hour then prayed asking God to draw closer to them. Haala and Adamma vowed to even get more serious with their prayer lives. They were seeing signs and wonders God had spoken about. Adamma sat in a chair and read the mid-week paper.

"Suicide victims, all ages end with 6. Much sympathy is extended to the families of those who lost their loved ones tragically through acts of suicide. When tragedies like these occur, the pain is hard to bear and requires much support from friends and families of these victims to pull through.

As she finished reading the paper, the words reverberated in her head.

Many persons are critical when others take their own lives, but we all have to remember that we are not supposed to be judgmental because we are not in the persons' shoes when they are suffering.

She further reflected that all the suicide victims ages were 16, 26 and 36. The second digits reminded her of the mark of the beast 666.

One week later, two more persons had committed suicide. Adamma Guidance was shaken to the core. She thought about the youth who was a Christian and yet hanged himself when the pressure was too great. She breathed a sigh of relief for the seven year old boy who had tried it, but was unsuccessful.

Sister Cairoshell's prophesy seemed to be fulfilled.

CHAPTER 17

Adamma Guidance was dressed half an hour before the street meeting that was to take place at Bridge Hill. Haala and Adamma were so excited with their walk with God that they were ever ready to support when the church was having a function. The extra time they had remaining, the two friends would use it talking and encouraging one another on their Christian pathway. Adamma waited for Haala to call so she could leave. It was a day she had looked forward to. As her phone rang, she answered.

"Ada, Gada Poise is by me."

Adamma remembered her from the last week newspaper. She was giving Hairounians a stern warning to repent of their sins before the wrath of God consumed them.

"Ada, I understand a lot of persons were mocking the woman and some were even saying she is crazy. Will Satan send somebody to warn people about their sins? I felt so sorry for the poor woman. Ada, I really feel it you know and she is also a sister in faith. Do you know what this reminds me of? The days of Noah when God told him to build an ark and the people were mocking him. They did not recognize their mistakes until it was too late! While I was in my kitchen preparing something for my family, the Holy Spirit told me to get in touch with her. I looked up the Poise in Mountain View, but I did not get her name so I called a Poise and I enquired how I could get in contact with her. Ada, God really good you know girl, you know the first number I called, that person was able to give me a number to reach her. She needs love and the Holy Spirit told me to invite her to my home and I could tell you that she is definitely a woman of God. I went out at the Bridge Hill Gap. I told her the clothes I was wearing. When she came out the bus, the Holy Spirit said to me, you need to hug her. I asked how it took so long to get here, girl Ad, she told me she was seeking the Lord to know if it was okay to come. She is a woman that strongly believes in pray. She is not doing things 'any and any how' and leaning on her own understanding. Well Ada what you could do, you could come by me and meet her, along with my Cousin Afafa and her daughter who I told you were coming from Trinity Island."

As she hung up the phone, Adamma Guidance was faced to make a sudden decision. Adamma was feeling reluctant. Deep within, she felt as though her friend made a decision in haste. Nevertheless, she decided to give her the benefit of the doubt. Adamma knew the prayer life they had and she remembered her friend saying the Holy Spirit had led her to invite the woman.

Adamma Guidance felt a deep, sudden urge to pray.

"God, I am your child. Heavenly father may you protect, guide and shield me. God, please don't be angry or look at me like "doubting Thomas," but God there are things I don't understand sometimes. Father, if by doing this I offend you please forgive me. Lord I also want you to search my heart and make it right. I find myself not moved with compassion like Sister Haala did for her fellowmen, but God if I am wrong forgive me and give me a heart like thine. Father let me be more compassionate. Let me trust you God and not doubt."

As she walked into her friend's yard, a litter of puppies was sucking their mother's breast. The door was opened.

They greeted her warmly and Haala took the opportunity to introduce her. They were reading the Bible and speaking about the goodness of God. When it was time to leave for the street meeting, Afafa and Gada offered to say a word of pray with Adamma. Gada's hand was holding Adamma's upper left arm only to release it quickly and called on Afafa to do the praying. Adamma was asked to pray to God silently to forgive her for any sins she would have committed. Quickly, Afafa anointed her forehead with oil. She prayed for God's blessings over Adamma's life and also his direction. As Adamma walked towards the street meeting all alone, she felt happy, free and at peace. There were so many people all around helping her along on her Christian pathway.

"Hello Ada it is me."

"Whats up?"

"Girl, you know Gada's sister and mother is by me also."

"Girl, what are you saying? What is your husband saying about all those people in your home?"

"Nothing. He seems cool about it. I want you to pray for me that he won't get vex or anything."

"Okay I will. Later then. I have some fish frying."

"Okay cool."

As she hung up the phone, Adamma spoke strongly to herself.

As a child of God, you really need to be more loving. I think you are really weak in that area. Why you have to be asking the woman what is her husband saying about all those people in her home? If she doesn't have a problem with it, why should you? You need to take page out of Haala's book.

CHAPTER 18

As Adamma Guidance stood at the side of the road awaiting a bus to go to school, she had to leap onto the side walk to escape a passing mini-bus. Ten minutes later, a brown van that was marked, 'Saturated' was approaching her. It was driven by an elderly man who was one of the few that drove cautiously. As she settled in the van, her cellular phone rang.

"Hello."

"Hello Ada, it is me. I am in my bedroom; I have to speak softly because I don't want them to think I am telling you everything. I called you to let you know we were at the hospital yesterday praying for the sick. While we were there, I heard Gada asked Afafa, Afafa what do you see? Afafa said she saw a man all in black going up the stairs of the hospital. From time to time she questioned Afafa and each time she responded and said what she saw. When we got home and were around the table eating, Gada confessed that she was testing to see if Afafa was indeed a true prophetess from God, but as Afafa revealed the things she was seeing, she realized she was real because she was also seeing the same things too. Gada said, at one point, Satan was trying to counter attack God's plan and confused her concerning Afafa."

"Oh okay. So she was testing to make sure she wasn't a wolf in sheep's clothing."

"Girl, yes so I said let me call you to tell you what was taking place. Enjoy your day at school today and take care."

"Thanks and later."

Even between God's messengers, Satan is pushing in himself Adamma thought.

As she walked onto the school's compound the bell rang loudly.

Six hours later, after a productive day at school Adamma dismissed her students and finally relaxed from the steady work she was doing.

CHAPTER 19

Looking at her time, Mrs. Guidance realized that if she didn't leave then, she will be late for church. Quickly, she stopped a bus and went to church. She was worried. Sister Haala is a person that is always early for church and if she was not going, she would have called.

As Adamma arrived at church, she joined the melodious singing. She was looking at the door regularly, but still there was no sign of Sister Haala. She checked her cellular phone, but there were no missed calls. Adamma listened as Sister Slater did the welcome.

"Dear friends, guests, brothers and sisters,

May I take this opportunity to welcome you here today at the Higher Calling Church. It is wonderful as always, to see all the familiar faces of our friends and all the special members of the congregation. I know that you all join me this morning in extending a heartfelt and sincere welcome to all our new converts. To our visitors, we want you to know that you have chosen the right place to be. We invite you with open arms to continue to come to our church because the doors are always wide open. If you have needs and want someone to listen and pray, we're here for you with open hearts and God's precious love to share away. May this ministry and its congregation offer you the opportunity to grow spiritually. As we celebrate under the theme: God, Health and Family Life, we trust that the message today will uplift and encourage you as we share together in fellowship. May our burdens be lifted, may you feel comforted and as the Lord reveals his plan and purpose in your precious lives, may you be inspired and encouraged to become active and involve in one of the many ministries that this body has to offer. Be encouraged with God's words: Isaiah 59 verse 19: When the enemy comes in like a flood the spirit of the Lord will lift up a standard against him. If we take an extremely close look at the story of Samson and the lion, we know the lion, Samson's enemy, came to destroy him, but instead with the help of the heavenly king, Samson was able to defeat his enemy. Now, when the lion was dead, he looked at the lion's carcass. In it was a swarm of bees and some honey, which he scooped out with his hand and ate. My dear brothers and sisters in Christ, God will bring honey out of a situation in which the enemy had meant to destroy your Life! God bless you and keep you may his great light continues to shine upon your beautiful face. Welcome one and welcome all.

Adamma Guidance stared at the door. Two hours later, as Sister Harry finished the health talk on the dangers of stress, Haala walked through the door. Adamma looked at the time, only to realize it was already eleven o clock.

"You had me so worried where have you been all this time?"

"Girl, I was praying for the person who is going to preach today. The Holy Spirit revealed to Afafa and Gada, the one who is going to preach is struggling a lot and needed praying for. The Lord has used me as the vessel to intercede on the person's behalf."

The service was over and members of the congregation greeted and chatted, Adamma waited as Haala spoke to few of the church members. As Sister Consuela came outside, Sister Haala greeted her and informed her that she was praying for the person who was going to preach.

"My dear sister thanks so much for praying for me. I needed that pray. I had such a rough week with so many trials that I did not know how I was going to preach. I felt as though I did not know where the strength was coming from. We have to build up each other in prayer."

Adamma looked as an emotional Sister Consuela hugged Haala tightly once again and walked away.

Forty minutes later, as she closed her door, Adamma Guidance knew without a doubt Afafa and Gada had a close relationship with God.

CHAPTER 20

"Hello," Adamma greeted.

"Girl I thought you and I like to read the Bible and pray, but Afafa and Gada beat us. Ad is every turn I turn these people are in their Bibles for tea, breakfast and dinner."

"Haala, once you truly have God anything is possible."

"True, true, while I was bathing today, I found myself thinking about the large lump sum of money God has promised my family. I am feeling so anxious to get it and I don't like the feeling because we are suppose to wait on God."

"I know what you are saying, if I was in your shoes I'd have looked forward to it as well, but you have to guard against being too thirsty."

"Exactly, that is why I want you to pray for me concerning the matter. I feel as though I wish I did not know."

"You had to know about it because the Lord doesn't do anything unless he speaks to his prophets. Remember his prophets are his mouth piece. Amos chapter 3 verse 7 says: Surely the Lord God will do nothing, but he revealeth his secret unto his servants the prophets. Whenever the Lord blesses you, Haala you will know the blessing came from the Lord and not of yourself."

"True. I understand what you are saying. We went prayer meeting today. It was wonderful. We spent a magnificent time glorifying and praising God and the Holy Spirit revealed to Sister Cairoshell that whenever Afafa and Gada have anything to say, Sister Cairoshell must allow them to say it. Sister Cairoshell also anointed them. Just before we leave to go to the prayer meeting Afafa told me many attempts were made to take my life and the Lord is going to bless me financially. Ada when I heard the revelations, I was so touched, all I could have done was to put my hands in the air and cried."

She heard her suddenly sucking her teeth.

"What is the problem?"

"Ada, people in this world could kill you for anything my sister. That is why we need God all the time. You know while Afafa and Gada were praying for my son the Holy Spirit revealed that a number of persons are jealous of him and a man who hates my husband with a passion is planning to attack him, but we prayed against it. They had to anoint him."

"My, my! but Lord Haala this is serious."

"The Lord also revealed my son is going to get all his subjects. Three ones and two twos."

"Is five he is doing right?"

"Yep."

"Ada, Afafa said you and I are very close friends. She said we are so close that there is only a small space left between for your husband."

Sitting in the dinning room, Adamma reflected on the conversation. She said a silent pray for Haala asking God to guard her heart and also the protection of her son.

Adamma Guidance always enjoyed going on the field to witness and distribute Priorities Magazines with her fellow believers. That particular day was no exception. She waited for her friend and her household. They took a bus and went to church.

As the groups were divided, many persons appeared to be skeptical thus leaving them all by themselves. This caused a great sadness to wash over Adamma.

As they walked into the Bridge Hill Gap, Afafa and Gada appeared humbled and undaunted by the circumstance. Adamma realized they have to be people who strongly believe in God because the ordinary man would have lashed back. They had an inner peace and strength. Ever so humble and with meekness Afafa spoke.

"Once you are following Jesus Christ, men are going to persecute you. Jesus the son of God went through persecution, who are us not to go through it as well? We have to remember we are not seeking men's approval. If we look at what the Bible says in Luke chapter 6 verse 26: Woe unto you, when all men shall speak well of you! If we also take a look at Luke chapter 22:63-65: It says: Men mocked Jesus and struck him. They even spat in his face. This is nothing we are facing in comparison to what Jesus went through. Look at John the Baptist who had gotten his head beheaded for righteousness sake and Stephen who was stoned to his death."

A calm smile crossed Afafa's lips. She shook her head at the dreaded situation. Adamma knew where the women were getting their strength; they were grounded in the scriptures.

In her heart, Adamma admitted God had chosen the ideal persons to do his job. Even though strong oppositions were coming their way, the women were courageously and faithfully carrying out the work of the Lord. They met a few persons whom they prayed with and distributed magazines.

They visited a female who is a close friend of Haala's. Everyone entered the house and took a seat except for Gada. Afafa was later called outside.

An eerie feeling came over Adamma.

"*Why these woman have to be out in the woman's yard for such a long time if they came to visit and pray. Stop being judgmental,*" *another voice accused.*

She reflected on the things they prophesied that came to pass. The very thought of what she was doing in silence pierced her heart. Silently, she looked around the house and thanked the Lord that no one could read her mind. It was between her and God.

Ten minutes later, Gada and Afafa returned. Everyone listened as Afafa spoke. "An evil seed was planted in your yard by someone who wishes to conquer the land. He comes into your yard at nights."

Don't even think they are lying because you fully well know they had asked Haala to pray for the person who was going to preach, because the person was having a rough time and right before your eyes, you have seen it unfolded. Look back at what Sister Cairoshell said, a lot of persons were going to commit suicide didn't you see it come to pass? You and your friend's main goal is to make it into heaven. You have gotten a dream that no one could have interpreted. Were those lies? No wonder the Bible says you are a generation of vipers. You are seeing the things right before your eyes, but yet still you want to doubt. Maybe, your mother should have named you 'doubting Thomas.' Somehow I believed she had given you the wrong name.

The lady broke down into bitter sobs. She held her head and cried, 'why nobody loves me.'

Afafa rubbed her back while informing her, God is still in control. Afafa had a sad expression on her face.

"The Lord said we must turn our Bibles to Isaiah 59 verse 19 it says: When the enemy comes in like a flood the spirit of the Lord will lift up a standard against him. My dear sister your enemy will never be able to touch you. The Lord will fight for you; he will lift up a standard against your enemy that is what the Lord is saying to you this afternoon."

Afafa sang loudly as the Holy Spirit moved upon her heart. She lifted her hands towards heaven.

"What a friend we have in Jesus,
All our sins and grief to bear;
What a privilege to carry.....

As Afafa finish singing, Gada informed her that the Lord said she had done well. Adamma Guidance felt like crying. It was the first time she ever heard that song sang in such a powerful and touching manner.

They were then asked to stand. As they stood, Adamma Guidance was commanded to sit and listen. At the command, she felt rejected by the God she loved. She was broken. Adamma was forcefully biting back the tears from falling. She knew she had to try much harder to be truly connected to God. It was as though they could have seen right through her. She knew it was the Lord who had instructed them. Nevertheless, as she sat and listened to their singing wild thoughts took over.

Lord, supposed these people sell me to the Devil as a sacrifice. God, remember you are a fair and a just God, you can't allow people to take innocent people to harm them right God?

As the session was over, Adamma directed a question to Gada.

"Why did I have to sit?"

"The Lord said these are the people he is going to use to form a choir." She pointed her right index finger at the others.

Girl, how can the Lord use you to form a choir when you have to go to school and teach, you are impossible and hard to go with eh. If it is one thing for a person who claimed to be a child of God, you really need to learn to behave yourself.

Gada later revealed that the Lord said he loves everyone and the curse that was placed in the lady's yard, the Lord has broken it."

Afafa then removed three wooden sculpted faces from the woman's wall claiming they will encourage evil spirits into her home. She informed the group that the faces are dead leaders from African tribes that were carved out as remembrance. Afafa firmly warned the woman that having those sculpted faces on her wall is like having other gods before Jehovah. They were then placed in a bag to be destroyed.

At ten minutes past seven in the night, the group left.

Adamma was deeply troubled.

Why does God send people with messages as such? A vision of the woman crying bitterly put in its appearance. *God it's as though you are traumatizing people.*

Adamma thought about all the good things they were doing, their humility and prophecies that were coming to past.

CHAPTER 21

"You are going to kneel and apologize to Leslie and please stop provoking the child. Grade five please remembered to walk with your net books. We have to see some pictures of the Caribs' Maboyas."

As Adamma Guidance opened the gate, Frisky licked her hand. The dog was so excited; it ran wildly around the yard then jumped consistently on her. She slipped into the house. Locking the door she peered outside. The pet was lying in front of the door with a deep frown on its face. Feeling guilty Adamma opened the door and patted Frisky on its head. She gave it an opportunity to jump on her. Walking through the hallway moments later, Adamma discovered the bathroom floor and the nearby bedroom were flooded. She felt like crying.

The ringing of the telephone took her mind from the current situation.

"Hello."

"Ada, how you are sounding so?"

"Girl my bathroom and bedroom flooded out."

"Oh Lord, girl I am sorry to hear that. Well I won't keep you long. God is good. You will get through."

"Thanks."

"My Cousin Afafa revealed that Gada's mother and sister used the compelling oil."

"What is that?"

"It is an oil that people used on their skin to control others."

"I never heard of that."

"Sister, when Gada sought the Lord, he revealed that what Afafa was saying was the truth. Gada told her mother and sister to their face they used the oil. She said the Lord said they must leave my home immediately for their great sin is an abomination unto him. Well Ada, I am not going to keep you any longer go mop and don't stress yourself. God is good."

Her confidence in them was restored. They were not compromising anything. Even though it was her sister and mother who were doing evil; Gada was exposing them boldly without favour. Adamma mopped with ease. She was no longer confused.

Well, you cannot say they are not speaking the truth now, because if they were lying is no way Afafa could have said those terrible things about Gada's relatives because that would have caused big, big confusion and separation.

CHAPTER 22

"Let us repeat the key thought," said Brother Padon adjusting his glasses.

"The book of Jonah reveals, among other things, that God is more willing to forgive others than we often are."

"Good, so today for our lesson study we will be looking at the Prophet Jonah. What really baffles me about this entire story is this, Jonah was given an instruction by God to warn Ninevah of a coming destruction, but instead of going where God sent him, Jonah ran away on a ship and headed to Tarshish" instead."

"Jonah disobeyed God because he knew God is a loving and forgiving God. In his heart he knew that God was going to forgive the people of Nineveh of their sins and within his heart Jonah figured after prophesying about a coming destruction to Nineveh and the prophecy does not come through, people were going to watch him as a liar and that was what he feared the most. We also have to remember Nahum called Nineveh was a blood city full of lies and robbery. (Nah 3:1) Jonah was sent to deliver God's message to such people. Perhaps it was also fear of the hated Assyrians, among other things, that prompted Jonah's attitude."

"Thank you Sister Logus for sharing with us, I want us to look closely at Jonah's attitude. For me I think Jonah was rebellious, selfish and stuck up. He was still in the ego-centric stage where it is all about him. He was not genuinely concerned about the wellbeing of others."

Brother Padon's statement drew a chuckle from Sister Logus. She raised her hand a second time.

"Yes Sister Logus, let us hear you."

"Even though all these things that you said about Jonah was true we have to remember," she was pointing a finger. "God would have seen something good about Jonah in order to use him as one of his prophets. We must also reflect on when Jonah was aboard the ship; the sailors have cast lots because they wanted to find out who was responsible for the storm. The lot fell on Jonah and he had asked the men to throw him over board in the raging sea. Now Brother Padon, it takes a certain kind of person to be willing to be thrown overboard. Even though Jonah had his weaknesses there were excellent things about him too."

"Very good Sister Logus your point is well taken."

A heated lesson discussion took place over Sister Logus' input. The bell was heard signaling the end of the lesson discussion.

Sister Haala and Adamma took a bus to go home. They confessed they had enjoyed the lesson study.

"Ada, you know yesterday at about six in the evening the Lord had impressed upon Afafa's heart that we must go into Surety Village. When I look at the time, the first thing that came to mind was, Lord how I am going to break this news to my husband. I said in my mind I will let the Holy Spirit lead. Sister when I approached my husband and told him, I was shocked to see he was okay about it. Ada you know Peter how he is so over protective, but the Lord just paved the way. Long ago, I couldn't go tell Peter those things and make it worst at that hour. As we traveled to Surety, I was wondering what we were going to see, but I said when I arrived I will see and behold with my eyes because I don't want to appear suspicious. Ad as soon as we came out the van, we saw a man with a cutlass cursing saying he was going to chop up some woman. You know when I approached the man? It was when Afafa and Gada calmed him. We prayed with him and girl soon after, the man started to speak about God. Sister that night we did not even go home. We went into a season of pray for the entire time. Girl, between you and I, when we get really tired and couldn't go anymore, we slept on cardboard boxes and when the morning cleared we came home."

"So you stayed out the entire night from your husband and son?"

"Girl yes and when I came back home, my husband did not ask me anything. I just went straight to the kitchen and made his breakfast. The Lord had prepared him so I could do his work."

As they departed, Adamma opened the door. Her heart was heavy. She looked around her big, comfortable house. She was grieved. Adamma knew without a doubt that she did not have the courage like Haala to leave her home and spent the entire night out doing God's work. Again, she questioned her standing with God. Adamma Guidance was feeling inadequate in comparison to the others. The sins of her heart were exposed. Sitting at the edge of her bed, tears were threatening to fall. Adamma was getting depressed. Her goal is to serve God, but she could clearly see there are things about her, she has to change. Sadly, she reflected on Sister Haala, even though she lived in a small home, she was walking with Jesus all the way no matter where he led her. Adamma was broken and with a sad countenance she reflected on the scripture reading that says: *'I say unto you, that a rich man shall hardly enter into the Kingdom of heaven. And again I say unto you, it is easier for a camel to go through the eye of a needle, than for a rich man to enter into the Kingdom of heaven.'*

Adamma Guidance was seeing a true reflection of who she really is. She was looking deep into her soul's mirror. Sorrows and great unhappiness were starting to take hold of her. Within she was feeling empty and helpless. Adamma knew God was showing her up, so she could be a better person, but the pain and void that came with it was severe. The tears that were threatening to fall were then falling freely.

CHAPTER 23

Even though God used others to expose her flaws, Adamma Guidance was destined to serve the Lord even though he pierced her. Adamma was seeking the Lord to give her a heart that was full of more love for him so she could serve him honestly without holding back. She was seeking the Lord with all her might to make her into the person he wanted her to be. However, she was unsatisfied with her current state and it troubled her greatly. She had never felt so unhappy, just the thought of knowing where she stood with the heavenly king, was a great torn in her flesh that was causing her great distress. Her once comfortable bed of peace had become one of torment at nights. Silently, she will lay awake and speak to God asking him to come closer to her, it was a great sorrow she had kept. She did not want others to know how she really stood with God. Adamma was suffering tremendously. The joy she had when she had given her life to Christ had slowly disappeared into thin air.

With a heavy heart, she picked up the ringing phone; Sister Haala spoke in an upsetting manner.

"As children of God, we must put on the whole amour or we will perish. We cannot have one foot in and one out."

"Sis what happened?"

"God revealed to my cousin the wicked things the people in our church are doing."

Adamma knew her friend thirsts for righteousness hence the reason for her to be severely upset.

"What things?"

"Baola and Kayin had sex twice. Thesharia and Faareh are using the compelling oil. They got it from a man named Salas. Sister Dibique's husband is cheating on her and she commanded the woman to kill herself. You remember when she had asked the church to pray for her?"

"Huh uh."

"Well her husband had given her a disease. Sister Maureenita is using a dildo and she is fantasizing about Brother Ayizie."

"Sister Haala this whole thing is sounding like gossiping. We have to exercise wisdom. Wisdom, wisdom is needed here."

"Ada, but you can't give me wisdom; is only Jesus Christ who could give me wisdom. God knows that I am giving him my all and you want to tell me he will send people to lead me away from him. Does that really make sense to you?"

"I am not saying that I could give you wisdom, all I am simply saying is for us to exercise wisdom."

Adamma, be honest with yourself and gave Jack his jacket and Mary her coat, you fully well know these people are speaking the truth, but your deepest fear is that you figure God will give them messages for you as well so you are trying to stop her before it get out of hand. Man, speak the truth. You fully well know your standing with God is a bit shaky, so you are trying to pervert the right ways of the Lord. Look at what you have become. You are nothing but a hypocrite.

Haala was speaking so loud and with great conviction that her cousin heard.

"Ada, my cousin said to look up Isaiah chapter 47 and verse 3 and Isaiah chapter 58 verse 1."

"Ada, you have to realize it is not what you think or what you want. It is about God. They can't compromise the word of God and talk nicely to suit people. They have to cry aloud just as God commanded them to do. They have to uphold the standard of God. Afafa said we must not attend service tonight because an evil spirit is covering the pastor. She said he is no longer leaning on God, but himself. She also said he used to deal."

The past tense struck Adamma like a bolt of lightning. *Lord why are you throwing someone's past into their face?*

"Watch, watch I hope you and your people are not forming the fool with my Christian pathway."

Look at the extent you have gone to. You are only putting up a front. Why you don't just accept the things for what they are.

"Ada, I am not that person and you fully well know that."

Adamma knew without a doubt, her friend was a honest person.

"By the way when can we go to church then?

"I don't know. The Lord did not reveal."

"What do you mean the Lord did not reveal."

"Okay, I will ask."

She waited until Sister Haala returned to the phone.

"We must stay away for two weeks."

"I don't understand this you know. How am I to know if your cousin is speaking the truth?"

"Well Ada for me, I will not be going because we are to follow what the Lord said. If you want to go you can go. Oh, I nearly forgot to tell you this, Sister Cairoshell had to cast out a demon from a woman because she was possessed. She also said, the Lord revealed a lot of persons are going to come to the prayer meetings that are demon possessed."

Her friend's words were weighing heavily on her mind as she hung up the phone moments later.

If you want to go, you could go, but I will not be going. You fully well know they are speaking the truth, but you are deliberately finding all sorts of excuses to prove them wrong when you know from deep within your heart it is the gospel truth. Can people be lying on people so and calling out their names so boldly? If they were not people of God then why are they pointing out sins? Soon, they will pick up on you and realized that you were just a fake.

She knew with all her heart, her friend would not harm her Christian pathway based on the relationship they had and their love for God.

She thought of Isaiah chapter 43:25: *I, even I, am he that blotted out thy transgression for mine own sake, and will not remember thy sins.*

As she sat in a chair Adamma spoke.

"Father you said we must come honestly to you because you know what is in our hearts. God I am getting sick and fed up with you. It is as though you are sucking the life out of me with a whole heap of revelations."

A few moments later, Adamma kneeled.

"Heavenly father, I am sorry to speak to you in that manner, but you are confusing me so much. Lord I know these people are speaking the truth because I have proven it so many times. Therefore, I cannot doubt and say it is not from you. God, I don't understand you. Why are you doing this Lord? Lord, what really hurts the most; you are not allowing the prophetesses to go to the people directly, you are exposing people. Lord, who really are you? Father I am speaking from the depth of my heart because you said come and let us reasoned together. God if I was Sister Thesharia and I knew that you told people those things about me, Lord I don't think I could ever serve you. Lord you are disgracing people and yet you want them to serve you. God, oh my Saviour, Jesus Christ of Nazareth, I am looking at you so differently. God in my eyes, you are not like the mighty God I once believed in. God, you are hurting me with the things you are doing. It is affecting me."

Placing her hands at her face Adamma began to cry, as thoughts took over her mind.

Girl, this is proof that God is not in existence. If God was really in existence and he was really whom he claimed to be, there is no way this could have been happening. How are you so sure, that there is really a God up above? Have you ever really seen him?

She read the scriptures that were given to her.

Isaiah chapter 47 verse 3: 'Your nakedness shall be uncovered, yes your shame will be seen; I will take vengeance and I will not arbitrate with a man.'

Isaiah chapter 58 verse 1: 'Cry aloud, spare not; lift up your voice like trumpet; tell my people their transgression and the house of Jacob their sins.'

The readings sent her even more into a serious state of depression. Adamma Guidance was fighting a great, challenging, serious spiritual battle that left her soul very bitter. Nevertheless, like a helpless child on that same day she spoke to God once more.

"Lord, even though I don't understand you at times, I still will trust you, but oh God help me to fight and pressed on."

Adamma thought about the lesson study they did on Amos where the people were getting fed up of him prophesying. It was a perfect example of her current state. She was just like the rebellious people in Amos' time.

No wonder they had to put you to sit down and you were not qualified for the choir because you won't let go and let God. You are fighting with all your might against God. I thought you said you loved him. Watch you! You are so fake.

As Sister Thesharia stood before the congregation to do the five minutes feature, Adamma found it difficult to focus on the words. Her thoughts kept drifting to the things she was doing in secret. She managed however to barely tuned in on few sentences.

"It will be terrible if a film was shown one day of the damaged our words have caused others. Many times, we do not think about the fact that the man, the woman, the person who speaks offensive, false, rude and inconsiderate words is like a mad man who throws firebrands, arrows and death." (Pro 26:18) Sarcastic and comic words are like death arrows that cut off life, or at least, dry up the existence of our fellowmen."

As Sister Maureenita appeared to carry on the song service, Adamma mind drifted to the things that were revealed about her. It was a great struggle to focus on the service. Every image of her fellow brothers and sisters in Christ were bringing back disturbing memories. Adamma Guidance's mind was properly programmed and controlled.

CHAPTER 24

At quarter past one in the morning, Adamma Guidance sat in the living room. She was having many sleepless nights. The great pressure of confusion was slowly destroying her. Many times her head felt as though it was going to split and shattered into a million pieces. At nights she tossed and turned, but sleep was never on her side. Her only faithful friends were heartache and pain. Adamma was losing faith in God. This particular night was no exception. As tears rolled down her cheeks, she questioned God.

"Why did you allow me to hear all these things about those people? Father if I am to die this moment, you are going to hold me accountable for thinking negative things about people; about things I don't even have proof off, yet still you allowed me to hear them. Lord you are not fair. It is a great hindrance on my path."

Even though Adamma was communicating with God, she wasn't feeling close to him as she once. There were things she didn't understand. Even though she forced herself with all her might not to look at God differently, she was fighting a losing battle. There was too much water under the bridge. She was pushing against the bricks and there were brutally, bruising and squeezing her.

A great wave of sadness came upon her. Adamma Guidance did not enjoy answering her telephone anymore. She was tired, frustrated and emotionally drained. Adamma knew her friend meant well. Walking into the kitchen, she bit a huge chunk of bread. She could no longer answer her phone without eating for fear her friend would pick up on her great sadness and look at her as though she didn't want to walk with the Lord.

"Hello."

"This early morning at six o clock, you are eating?"

"Bread." She muttered the single word and continued to chew.

"God is a romantic God you know. God revealed to Gada how I must make love to my husband so I am passing it on to you. She said when I am making love to him, I must pass my hands in his sweat, massage his temples and kiss him on the lips and tell him I love him, but God loves him more. Ad, she also revealed some things about your life, when I heard it, I cried. We need to talk in private."

There was a pause.

"Things like what?"

"We would see to talk."

Moments later, they hung up the phone. Adamma drifted off into thought. This was the final blow and it was as though she was expecting it.

God, God what are you doing to me? God, God what are you doing? God, you are messing up!

As Adamma Guidance and her husband made love, Haala's voice was ringing in her head.

God is a romantic God you know. God revealed to Gada how I must make love to my husband so I am passing it on to you. She said when I am making love to him, I must pass my hands in his sweat, massage his temples and kiss him on the lips and tell him I love him, but God loves him more. Ada she also revealed somethings about your life. We will see to talk in private.

It was a serious disturbance. Nevertheless, she forced with all her might to push her words aside and concentrate and making her husband happy. Adamma fought a losing battle. On a number of occasions, as her husband tried to make love to her, Adamma Guidance was shutting down. Her relationship and marriage with her husband was starting to be affected severely.

One week later, Adamma reluctantly picked up the annoying telephone. She knew she couldn't ignore it forever.

"Ada, I thought you were not home, I almost hang up. At the prayer meeting yesterday, Sister Cairoshell revealed a lot of persons are going through sexual dysfunction."

After hanging up the phone moments later, Adamma Guidance spoke to God.

"God, you are painting such a lovely picture of yourself. Why are you doing this to me God?"

Adamma paced her home. She was wounded. Nevertheless, she was forcing to stick with God no matter what. With tears rolling down her face, Adamma spoke.

"God though you slay me, I will serve you. Lord, hold my hand for I am facing my darkest hours on earth. I begged of you to hold my hand."

Even though she had made a promise to the Lord to serve him till the end, Adamma was slowly drowning. She was barely hanging on by a thin thread. Once every month she attended church. Some of the members had jokingly nicknamed her stranger. Adamma Guidance smiled as though it was cool, but inside she was a damaged, broken woman. She was at a point in her life, where she had no idea where to turn. Adamma felt downcast, depressed and ready to give up. All her emotional strength was gone. She was completely drained. Her spiritual experience seemed non-existent. Mrs. Guidance felt as though her prayers were falling to the ground. She had sunk to the lowest point in her life. Mrs. Adamma Guidance had hit rock bottom. She was facing a time of tremendous despair.

CHAPTER 25

Haala was going to church regularly. She was unaffected by the entire ordeal. Through her window, Adamma could see her in a broad white hat and a four inch high heel holding her son's hand as they waited for a bus. As the wind blew, she held her multi-coloured dress.

Even though she did not have the courage to attend church at times, she would reason with God.

A few hours later, at one o' clock, her cellular phone rang.

"Hello Ada, you at home?"

"Yes."

"I am calling you, but your house phone kept on ringing."

"Let me check."

As she walked into the study, she noticed the cord had slipped out.

"Hey Haala, the cord had slipped out."

"Oh, okay that was the problem. Ada I got a dream about us last night and one night before. From our hymnal I dreamt we were singing page three hundred and thirty one and after we were finished, you were prophesying and saying a lot of people houses are going to be burnt and night before, I dreamt you came into my yard and said you wish you could be just like me. Ada, you must buy a bottle of olive oil and let me anoint you and put you back on your Christian pathway. Sister Cairoshell said I have the gift of healing."

Adamma could hear Haala's husband calling her urgently in the background.

"Ada later, I am going to see what my hussy wants." As she turned the pages of her song book to three hundred and thirty one, Adamma read the words.

Oh Jesus, I have promised
To serve thee to the end;
Be thou forever near me...

As she finished reading the song, tears bathed her cheeks. Adamma remembered the serious vow she had made to God a long time ago, but was finding it impossible to keep. She found herself meditating deeply on the words.

Sister Haala would encourage her to go more often to church, but Adamma Guidance was already spiritually wounded. Adamma was trying to reach out to God, but it was so difficult to reach him when he was hurting her so much. Her heavenly father she had looked up to has appeared as though his loving arms were filled with bob wires. Every time she made a step towards him, it was as though he was gashing her. She was like a bird with broken wings in hiding trying to nurse her wounds. Adamma found herself fleeing from the very presence of God.

CHAPTER 26

A few minutes past twelve Mrs. Guidance marked the last book. She picked up her lunch from the table, and walked over to the nearby house where she usually ate lunch. This was a norm to get some peace during her lunch break. A couple times, she had tried eating at school, only to be disturbed consistently with complains. As she walked into Miss Peters' yard, she met her conversing with another woman in her porch. Adamma said, "good afternoon" and took a seat to eat her lunch.

"*I didn't know how that woman did not kill herself. She dashed herself over a steep bank like that and ran straight into a pig pen exposing her naked buttocks.*"

"*But Miss Peters it is a lucky thing my daughter's husband was at home because I don't know how she was getting to the hospital.*"

"*I wasn't even worry about her so much. Is her poor little daughter I was so scared for when she looked at her mother in the pen and was crying.*"

"*But she said she is a prophetess, girl I couldn't help but laugh when the pig ran away with her hat.*"

"*Miss Peters later girl. I see you have company so we will catch up later.*"

"*Okay Marcy walk good.*"

As soon as the other woman stepped onto the main road, Miss Peters spoke.

"Mrs. Guidance we had one big show down here on Saturday. Miss if you see a crowd of people you

might think it was a carnival. There is this woman who
went to Nothing Hill crusade Friday night and miss, she
practically mashed up the crusade. She was revealing a
number of things. Mrs. Guidance, come with me behind
my house. I have something to show you. You see that
high bank over there?" the woman pointed.

"Huh uh."

"Miss Guidance on Saturday, the woman dashed
herself over that bank and ran straight into Miss Marcy
dirty pig pen. She lay down in there spread out. Her
skirt rose up and everybody could see her naked, fat
bottom. Out of place 'old boy' said, he didn't have to get
sex for a whole week because his eyes already fatten."
With her eyes opened big, Adamma asked Miss Peters
the woman's name.

"Afafa is her name and so she figure she knows the
Bible more than everybody. The whole bunch of them
sick even the skinny one that does be walking with her
saying they prophesying. I think she came from some
where in Mountain View. Is exposed God exposed her,
that is why she found herself in the pig pen bare bottom.
God is angry at them because they are deceiving so
many people."

As she took off her shoes, Adamma's face was burning. Never had she felt so angry and betrayed. With shaking fingers, she dialed Sister Haala's number.

"I thought you were my friend, but you have deceived me!"

"Ada, Ada what is happening what is going on?"

"You know your cousin is demonic and you deliberately led me into a trap and let her anointed my forehead. You said I was your friend. The whole of Nothing Hill have your sick cousin's name on the street saying that she was bare bottom in a pig pen."

"You don't approach me in that manner and in that temper. So what happen if my cousin rubbed a drop of oil on your forehead? Will it kill you? No woman was in any pig pen bare bottom, but commonsense can't tell you that was all a lie. They are just against the woman. You just go and find out your facts straight. Right about now, I already have too much on my plate."

At her friend's remarks, Adamma hung up.

Girl, using your own commonsense, you actually believe that Afafa was bare bottom in a pig pen? You fully well know that the woman must have been rebuking them from their sins and they got angry and 'cook up' something on her. You see you, if you are not careful, you will end up just like Judas. Now, you are really seeing a true reflection of yourself. You see, sometimes

God has to use other people to really help us. Hmmn, once you had really believed you were close to God, only to realize it wasn't so at all. Look at the extent you have gone to now, believing Afafa was bare bottom in a pig pen. Girl, you've got to be careful. Be very careful you don't end up being a deceiver of your own self.

CHAPTER 27

"Mrs. Guidance, you expect a big woman like me would just be telling lies on people so. Watch me just walk around the road and asked anybody what took place at Nothing Hill Saturday? I told you here was like a Carnival. The woman ended up in Marcy's pig pen with her bottom exposed. Don't bother with her, she would cover up for her cousin," said an angry Miss Peters ready for confrontation.

As she took off her high heels and placed them on the mat, Adamma Guidance picked up the ringing phone.

"Ada," her friend said ever so gently.

"Yes."

"I spoke to my cousin concerning what you said yesterday and she told me yes it was the truth, but I couldn't call you back because of the rage you were in. She said it was when the Lord revealed to her, the condition of the church at Nothing Hill is when she ran over the bank and into the pen. The people are living such an ungodly life."

"Haala your relative is a wicked woman!"

"Adamma be very careful what you say about God's people! A prophet in the Bible had walked naked. You think being a prophetess is an easy task? Prophets have to bear the Lord's burden. They do go through a lot of trying times! My cousin said to tell you read Isaiah chapter 20. I don't know if that would help."

Not wanting to have any more conversation with Haala and still angry Adamma hung up the phone. Adamma reflected on Haala's cousin admitting she was bare bottom in a pig pen. She drifted further into thought. *It takes a honest person to admit something as such. Boy, if she was really working with the enemy she would have hid that pitfall at all cost. Girl, remember you personally did not see her, it is people who told you about what took place so she could have easily denied it, but she didn't. Girl, there is some truth to this thing.* Adamma reasoned to herself as best as she could.

She turned her Bible to Isaiah chapter 20.

In the year that Tar'-tan came unto Ash'-dod (when Sar'-gon the king of As-syr'-i-a sent him,) and fought against Ash'-dod, and took it;

At the same time spake the Lord by Isaiah the son of Amoz, saying, go and loose the sackcloth from off thy loins, and put off thy shoe from thy foot. And he did so, walking naked and bare-foot.

And the Lord said, like as my servant Isaiah hath walked naked and barefoot three years for a sign and wonder upon Egypt and upon Ethiopia;

So shall the king of As-syr-i-a lead away the Egyptians prisoners, and the Ethiopians captives, young and old, naked and barefoot, even with their buttocks uncovered, to the shame of Egypt.

And they shall be afraid and ashamed of Ethiopia their expectations, and of Egypt their glory.

And the inhabitant of this isle shall say in that day, behold, such is our expectation, whither we flee for help to be delivered from the king of Assyria: and how shall we escape?

She read over the portion of scripture a third time. It was the first she was encountering that scripture. Once again, she was thrown into a state of confusion only worst than before.

God, who are you? Adamma reflected on the dream Sister Haala told her, about her prophesying.

If you think you God is going to make me a prophetess and have me in that condition, I have shocking news for you. Keep your spiritual gift. I don't want it! God, I don't mean to be disrespectful, but it appears as though you are doing a whole bunch of stupidness. God, is only forcing I am forcing myself to follow you right about now, and if you don't stop this "thing" you are doing soon, I won't be able to walk with you. Lord, I am going to be honest with you. Walking with you is extremely bitter and painful. Lord, how long do you think I could walk on broken bottles and not give up? God you are tempting and pushing me with all your might to rebel against you, but only because I know you are God is the only reason I am still holding on.

Okay God I am sorry, I was disrespectful. Lord, your words said for my thoughts, are not your thoughts, neither are your ways my ways, declares the Lord. As the heavens are higher than the earth, so are my ways higher than yours and my thoughts than yours. God, I just want you to know this, I just can't see you through this. I just can't, it doesn't matter how hard I tried. I really don't understand. I am totally surrounded by darkness.

CHAPTER 28

Adamma was keeping a far distance from Haala, her family and friend. Even though Sister Haala would call and Adamma missed the calls, she would not return them. She was scared and confused. Her home has become one of torment. Just to get away, Adamma would go at her aunt's home at Malibu. In her closet, she was continually questioning God. Many times, she felt like totally giving up. The battle was going on too long and was getting even more challenging. At times she felt she was going to fall. Many times at school, she lay on her desk when the pressure was too great.

One day as she came from school and couldn't bare the pressure any longer, she telephoned Sister Haala and told her how she was feeling. Sister Haala had asked if she ever tried to fight what the Lord said and she admitted. She informed Adamma that Satan is wrestling strongly with her to confuse her mind to cancel out what God had said that was why she was feeling that way. Sister Haala prayed a powerful pray with her, then told her of a dream she had with both of them.

"I dreamt we were going on a journey. I was walking forward and you were walking backward and you were encouraging me to walk like you."

"I don't like that dream. That was not a nice dream," was all Adamma could have said sadly.

As she came off the phone, Adamma went down on her knees and cried out in anguish to God.

"Father, if I have hurt you by not listening to you, please be merciful to me. I guess that is why my pain is so hot. Lord I do accept everything your prophetesses said, everything God."

Adamma reflected on the dream Sister Haala told her. She knew within her heart she was trying to get away. She just couldn't face the hard facts of life. The sadness in Haala's voice reverberated in her head. She knew she was hurting as well. Being an honest and fair person Adamma spoke.

"Father, God search me because you know me even more than how I know myself and Lord if I am a stumbling block in Haala's Christian pathway, Lord please take my life, don't let me be a hindrance to anyone. Take my life God! Take it. I could no longer live like this God. This is too much suffering and soon, I am feeling as though I will crumble."

Even though she asked the Lord to let her accept what his prophetesses said, Adamma Guidance found it a bitter pill that just won't go down her throat or if it did, it forced its way up.

It was Haala's and Adamma's turned to lead the song service. As they walked to the pulpit, Adamma walked a safe distance. She listened as Haala called out the first song to the congregation.

It was a song Adamma did not know, but had to listen, so she could pick up and tune in.

I will follow thee my Saviour,
Wheresoe'er my lot maybe.
Though all men should forsake thee,
By the grace I'll follow thee.

Tears made its way slowly down Haala's cheeks. Even though she was feeling sorry, Adamma Guidance was still keeping a safe distance.

As she entered her home, Adamma focused on the words of the song. It touched the core of her heart.

*Look at how you are treating your once close friend.
I am one hundred percent sure that woman would have
given her right hand for you. You are hurting that
woman real bad. Look at how she was crying during
the song service. She knows you are distancing yourself
from her. Anytime you needed help, she was always
there. Look back at the time when you were at Step-Up
Teachers College and you had an assignment to take in
and when you were about to print it off, the computer
froze. When you called that woman and you told her
you were in distressed, she was crying her heart out to
God for you as though she was naturally feeling your
pain. Even when you had clothes to wash that woman
was leaving her home and out of love, she was helping
you. Oh God, like you don't even have a conscience.
You only look so, but you are a wicked woman.*

Adamma was literally torn into two. It was as though
they were grinding her into fine powder. If she distance
herself from her friend because of the unbearably pain
it was causing, her conscience will not let her have any
peace it was chastising her brutally and if she tried
holding to her friend, it was like sharp, broken bottles
sinking very deep into her flesh causing her great harm.
To survive the tremendous pressure, a deeply bruised
and wounded Adamma had to immediately apply her
survival skills. She had no other choice, but to stay

away from church. Adamma was wise enough to know she had to shield herself by blocking some of the immeasurable pain. She had to stay down if she wanted to continue to be a healthy individual. A great down fall was banging at her door, but she was a fighter, she was still clinging to God even though she knew fully well she was going under. Adamma refused to let go and fall even though it had appeared as though God was not on her side. She was going down with God on her lips. She was not letting go off him, she was wrestling with him severely for deliverance of the unknown. Adamma adamantly refused to accept defeat, like a wounded, bleeding soldier on the front of a battle field; she was holding her ground even though she knew she must surrender it would be easier that way. Adamma was in an extremely fragile state. She was traumatized to the extreme.

Her storm was threatening to drown her, if God don't intercede then, Adamma Guidance was going under with a terrible blow that would alter her life forever. Her feet were already slipping. The angry waves were blasting, beating and crushing her, but with feeble hands she was still holding on to the rock even though the rough swells were slamming against her hands and trying to push them off.

CHAPTER 29

A number of parents were already on the outside waiting on Mrs. Guidance. It was open day at the school, where parents would come and speak to the teachers concerning their child's attitude and performance. As she sat at her desk speaking to a parent concerning her son and looking over his records, out of the corner of her left eye, she could see a woman standing ever so near her window staring at her intently.

Lord, I can't take any more of this pressure. God what happen to you? I thought you said you don't give a man more than he could bear. God, can't you see I am going to fall before your eyes and you are not helping me. Father why do you turn a blind eye when I need you the most? Is it that you don't love me anymore? God, I am going to be honest with you, if I succumb to this pressure, honestly I don't think I could ever serve you again. What about the times I had served you faithfully? Have you forgotten those times? Jehovah, I am feeling strongly as though you are not in existence. Am I serving a helpless God? I have given you my all God, my all, but you have failed me.

Adamma was forcefully biting back tears. A strong pressure was mounting within her as though it wanted to shatter her. She could clearly see she was not going to make it. There was no strength left in her to fight anymore. Her body was giving up on her. Adamma was in a position in which she just couldn't handle anymore stress. She could tell this was the final blow to sink her.

You were talking about you were serving God till the end; you will get up and go outside to face your calamity. If you had never given your life to God this would have never happened to you. Let your God help you through this one. That good for you!

Lord, are you going to let me regret that I have given my life to you. Are you going to cause me to look back at my life and think there is no help for me in God?

Suddenly, the woman started weeping.

"Miss Justin! Miss Justin!" on hearing the woman crying, Adamma asked the parent for an excused. She wondered fearfully if she had given the woman's son Justin a hard time and he had complained her. As she came in close contact with the woman she then heard clearly what she was saying.

"Miss trust him, miss trust him, trust God alone don't trust anybody."

The strange woman held onto her hands and wept. It was as though she could see and feel her pain and confusion. Mrs. Guidance turned her face away for a long moment to avoid crying.

"Seek and you shall find. Knock and the door shall be opened." The woman strongly warned her twice.

As Adamma made an attempt to question the woman, she left claiming she had to go to work. As she dealt with the other parents, the strange woman's voice kept playing in her head.

Two weeks later, as Adamma Guidance walked down the steps to her classroom. She saw a woman looking just like the woman who would have spoken to her, as she enquired she realized, she was seriously mistaken. Many times she tried to locate the woman, but have never seen her face on the school's compound.

CHAPTER 30

As Adamma Guidance sat at her desk, she reminded the noisy grade five students that it was time for silent reading.

"Miss," called Tyreke.

"Yes."

"Can I read a story to the class?"

"Sure."

As Tyreke came out of his seat, he stood in front of the class with his story book.

"Tyreke get a bench and sit. You would be more comfortable."

Mrs. Guidance listened to the story. From deep within she felt as though that story was meant for her. She reminisced on the content.

A king was bitter and angry with God, because he had cut off his finger. One day, the king was captured in the woods by some men and was about to be offered to their god as a sacrifice, but when they saw his hand, they released him immediately because the tribe deity would not accept the offering of a handicapped. His cut finger had saved his life.

As Mrs. Guidance climbed the steps, she focused on the story her student did. She repeated the moral. *"Whatever happens, happens according to God's will."* Adamma applied it to her life. There must be a reason she was going through this storm. One day, some day soon, she would be able to look back and realized the reason God would have allowed her to go through such a terrible time.

You fully well know that this storm is going to drown you, but you are behaving as though there is hope.

Look at you, can't you see with your eyes how fragile you have become. Adamma, it is only a matter of time before you fall apart, only a matter of time. Look at the severe back pain you are having your body is trying to fight of the stress, but how long do you think your body can function under such tremendous pressure? You are already on the brink. Even a fool could see it, but you are so stubborn.

Two days later, Adamma picked up her ringing telephone.

"Ada, your right foot does give you problem?"

"Why you asked that?"

"I dreamt your right foot was swollen and Sister Cairoshell was praying over it down at a seaside."

Not wanting to hold a long conversation with Sister Haala, Adamma informed her she had to wash. As she hung up the phone, Adamma's mind drifted for a moment.

"Hmmmn seems like somebody is in serious training."

She looked down at her right foot. It was hurting her a few days ago. She thought about the dream Sister Haala had told her about her coming into her yard and saying she wish she could be just like her. *Everybody has to know what they are doing. Father, God where she got that dream from? Lord, could you tell me what is really happening?*

Tears ran down her cheeks. Feeling extremely confused and needing help desperately, Adamma decided to do some research on the internet. From deep within she was having serious doubt that God would actually allow one of his prophets to walk naked, even though she read it.

Half an hour later, after composing herself, Adamma sat in front the computer and researched Isaiah chapter 20.

It clouds ones imagination to believe that God will allow Isaiah, one of his prophets to walk absolutely naked and barefooted for three years, not even wearing a jockey. Is this the quality of God we serve? Surely not.

These foregoing comments are perfect examples of twisting of Bible verses. It simply means that Isaiah would put off the outer sackcloth and keep the inner vest. This is an indication that Egypt would lose its possession if the people fail to repent.

As she continued her research, she found some interesting readings about false prophets.

Money is always a part of their message. By greed, they manipulate people by deceiving them with prophecies of blessings. A true prophet sent by God must be 100% accurate. There is absolutely no room for errors. There is no such thing as a prophet learning to prophesy or a prophet in training.

Adamma Guidance went to sleep with a clear head. She was putting her demons to rest.

CHAPTER 31

A few months later...

Adamma Guidance paid the secretary for the three different newspapers. As soon as she tucked them into her bag, she took a bus and went home. Putting her clothing in the basket that stood in the corner of the room and putting on a cotton dress, she lay on the bed and scanned one of the papers. Adamma looked at the names and photos of the students who were outstanding at their CSEC exams.

Feeling as though sleep was about to over power her, Adamma briefly went through one of their achievements.

Gutter gained grade one in Biology, Caribbean History, Chemistry, English A, English B, French, Geography, Information Technology, Mathematics, Physics and Social-Studies. Feeling exhausted Adamma fell asleep with the paper in her hand.

Two days later, Adamma picked up her phone.

"Hello."

"Hello, Ada it's me. My son did not get all his subjects. He got three. I am thinking about sending him back to school. I am not discouraged or anything. I am continuing to serve the Lord because I honestly love him."

Realizing her friend was just trying to pass off the conversation as smooth as silk, Adamma got highly annoyed.

"You see me right about now, I need my space. This phone calling thing, I really can't handle it anymore."

It was the last bit of information she needed to fit the puzzle perfectly together to explain her life shattering experience.

Deuteronomy chapter 18 verse 22 went off like a loud alarm in her head. "***When a prophet speaketh in the name of the Lord, if the thing follow not, nor come to pass, that is the thing which the Lord hath not***

<u>spoken, but the prophet hath spoken it presumptuously thou shalt not be afraid of him.</u>

As she sat at her kitchen table, Adamma reflected on all the torment she went through with those dangerous people. She focused her mind on Sister Haala; she remembered the dreams she had brought to her that sank her into depression. Adamma also reflected on the good times they had together. It was impressed upon her heart, to speak to her friend face to face.

As they stood at the back of the Higher Calling Church, Adamma spoke. "Right about now I'm feeling angry! Haala, Afafa is your cousin you must have known something about her!"

"No, I wasn't aware she was that kind of person."

"How could you not know anything about your own family?" You must have known something!"

"I heard things about her, but you know sometimes; you want to really see if they are true." "But you could have at least say something to me and you didn't, that was wrong and what hurts the most, is having a person as such putting oil on people's forehead. You have deceived me! You have led me into a dangerous trap of which you had knowledge of."

She looked as Haala folded her skirt between her legs and tapped both her powerful hands on the concrete wall. She looked long and hard into clear, blue sky.

"Okay, I am sorry." As Adamma continued to lash out, Haala stooped and cried with all her might. She was heard saying these words, "Lord, I can see the humbleness this morning. I can see the humbleness and meekness Lord. Father I thank you for bringing me thus far on my Christian pathway."

Her crying made Adamma even more upset.

"As far as I am concerned, you just like a big hypocrite! Where did you get all those lying, disastrous dreams from to tell me? I strongly believed that you are one of them too! You fully well know that light and darkness cannot go together, but yet still you are still going at Sister Cairoshell's demonic prayer meeting. When you fully well know that Sister Cairoshell would have told your cousin that the Lord said, that whatever your cousin Afafa and Gada have to say she must allow them. How is that possible? It means that they are seeking the same source. Isn't that a clear cut situation? The Bible tells us in 2 Corinthians chapter 6 verse 14: **'<u>Be ye not unequally yoked together with unbelievers: for what fellowship hath righteousness with unrighteousness? And what communion hath light with darkness?'</u>**

"No, no I am not one of them, Ada honestly I got those dreams. I would never lie to you in that manner. Ada to be honest with you, I am feeling confused about this whole situation because a lot of persons are going there and even some pastors' wives. Ada, but you could also know when people love the Lord. Sister Cairoshell has a deep love for God and I could naturally see it."

"But you can't look at the pastors' wives. Look at yourself. You have the missing pieces to the puzzle and you are still going to the prayer meeting. In your case you have no excuse! What happen, you want God come down from heaven and tell you they are counterfeits? What more evidence do you want?

There was a long silence.

"Ada, you have to remember too that you were the one who told me about Sister Cairoshell."

"Haala, Haala, I know exactly what you are doing. You fully well know you cannot hold me responsible for telling you about her because at the time, I had no knowledge that she is a false prophetess. She is a sister in faith. I wasn't expecting that from her. I know the Bible spoke about false prophet rising from within, but it just took me by surprise. It would have been almost impossible to detect her if it weren't for your cousin Afafa and Gada. She is more subtle, wiser and composed. If God did not cause our paths to cross how would I be able to expose her as a false prophetess? Can I speak about something that I know absolutely nothing about?"

At her last two questions, Adamma could see Haala shaking her head defensively in defending Sister Cairoshell as a true prophetess. She however admitted that Gada and Afafa were false, but by attending Sister Cairoshell's prayer meeting they could come to true repentance. She also spoke highly of loving one another and forgiveness drawing reference to how our heavenly father loves us with an unconditional love. Haala further stressed she was happy that she housed them in a time when everyone seemed to be against them because amidst it all, she realized they are still God's children.

"You are just simply finding all sorts of disgusting excuses to be with them. If God revealed himself to you, you need to get out from there! I will always remember the good times we had as prayer partners."

"I have asked God to let you remember the good times and not only the bad times."

Adamma looked as Haala leaned her head against the wall and looked far out into space as tears flowed uncontrollably down her face.

"It is hard to sweep the good times under the carpet. I won't and I am sorry to call you a hypocrite."

"It hurt me when you called me a hypocrite."

"I am sorry."

Slowly and sadly, they walked back into the church, keeping a safe distance. Adamma could see clearly Haala was set in her ways. For Adamma it was difficult knowing whom to trust. Silently, she thought about the times she had cried and Haala was there helping her along in earlier times of their friendship.

Lord, how will I ever be able to trust her again? Father, look at all the dreams she brought me, all of them were dreams that joined forces with the enemy. God, you are not a foolish God, you have created the human minds and you know exactly how humans think. Into your hands Lord I have placed her, may you deal with the situation accordingly. All things that are broken, God, you can fix them.

CHAPTER 32

Adamma sat at the back of a crowded bus, next to a window. She was going into Queenstown, to buy some tokens for her students who did well in their test. As the bus arrived at the Bridge Hill Gap, Adamma saw a faithful Haala dressed all in white awaiting a bus to attend the prayer meeting. The strange woman who came at her school voice reverberated through her head. *"Miss, don't trust anybody. Trust only God."*

Lord, how could she not see something is definitely wrong with the prayer meeting?

As Adamma confided in Sister Efia, it was then discovered that Sister Efia had encountered Sister Cairoshell. She had revealed that Sister Efia has a disobedient son and a cyst on her womb. Her revelations were true.

Adamma strongly reminded Sister Efia that Satan will work miracles. He will make people sick and then will suddenly remove from them his satanic power. They will then be regarded as healed. If we are not careful as God's children, we could fall victims to the lying wonders of the enemy. The working of marvelous miracles by the antichrists is what is going to really test and shake our faith as Christians.

Sister Efia had also informed Adamma she had met with Sister Haala and some others who attended the prayer meeting and by talking, one of the women reminded Sister Haala of the prayer meeting that was to take place on Saturday from eleven am to two pm. This was the first time Sister Cairoshell was having a prayer meeting on Saturday. Sister Efia and Adamma realized instantly that Sister Cairoshell was testing to see how much of the people were ready to attend prayer meeting on that particular day in which they were suppose to attend another church.

As the sisters made an attempt to speak to Sister Haala, about her danger, she cried loudly, held her right hand in the air and said, "I love the Lord! God, if you know I am displeasing you by going to the prayer meeting, cripple me God if you have to, cripple me God because I honestly want to serve you." She went down on the ground and sobbed. Sister Efia had to hold her into her hands to calm her.

"I know you love the Lord Haala, but you have been deceived."

"No, no, no when I am at the prayer meetings, I could naturally feel the presence of the Lord. Sister Cairoshell is a woman of God." As soon as she finished speaking, she continued to cry like a woman who has been provoked.

"But Sister Haala, you must learn to listen. The scriptures are there to guide us and you are deliberately ignoring them," warned Adamma.

It was as though Adamma stepped on splinters.

"You are operating as though you are God! It is like you want to take the position of God! If I am to move from the prayer meeting, I will move in God's time. Allow God to do his work! God is the judge not you. All you are doing is judging people. Are you God? Right about now, more and more I am realizing I have no friends. I am standing all alone! No one knows what I am going through all because I have made a serious decision to go with Christ all the way! All I want to do is to make it into heaven! Oh God, I just want to make it into he..aven!" She yelled in anger and continued crying.

Adamma could see Haala blowing heavily. She was brutally upset and tired.

A few passersby looked worriedly in their direction.

At her statement, Adamma reflected on the revelation Sister Cairoshell made concerning Haala. *She was indeed a very strong pillar to the prayer meeting.* Adamma knew one thing in her heart, if she does not stand firm on the word of God these people will definitely topple her over.

She thought of Acts chapter 20: 29-31: "*For I know this, that after my departing shall grievous wolves enter in among you, not sparing the flock. Also of your own selves shall men arise, speaking perverse things, to draw away disciples after them. Therefore watch, and remember, that by the space of three years I ceased not to warn everyone night and day with tears."*

As Adamma got home, she sat in a chair and rubbed her forehead. Her head was spinning and hurting. She was forced to do some reflections. Her mind raced back to the years Haala and her had spent glorifying God and trusting each other. Image of her friend going down to the ground in agony and crying bitter tears put in its appearance. Quickly, she pulled her Bible and went over the scriptures on false prophets. The tide needed her and it was coming in extremely strong.

You saw how Haala was behaving; you have to leave that woman alone. It appears as though they are using her as the bait to get you, you have to stand firm on the word of God. You have to embrace the word of God for what it is. She is trying her utmost to pull you with her and it does not matter what you told her before, she's set in her ways. You have got to run like hell. Let her cry and behave with her 'antics.' You have got to get out her way. You are no match for the enemy. Satan will go to the extreme to get want he wants. Above all things, God understands. Do not feel guilty or hurt because you are distancing yourself from her and you no longer speak to her on the phone. God knows if you try to continue on that path, you would never be the same again. These people are extremely wicked. There are certain things you cannot deal with, you just have to leave it in the hands of the most high. This war is too dangerous for you. These people will grind you to ashes. Sometimes, you have to save yourself in order to help someone.

CHAPTER 33

As Adamma Guidance stepped into the bathroom, she heard her cellular phone made a sound. The red light was blinking. Sister Haala was constantly sending her messages even though Adamma was keeping a safe distance. Even though she had pointed out to Sister Haala that it is impossible Sister Cairoshell could be a true prophetess, she was failing miserably to accept the plain truth. Every time she sent a text, she was slipping in something from what Sister Cairoshell revealed at the prayer meeting.

A few minutes later, Adamma read the text.

"Good morning,

I want you to know, I don't have any hatred, grudges or unforgiveness towards you. I still love you and you are still my friend, but it seems like you don't want to walk with me from church. I have no problem with that. All I want to do right now is to please God and intercede on others behalf. A lot of husbands are cheating on their wives. You need to pray for your family. I've been accused and judged wrongfully, but I thank God for the many trials in my life there help me to grow closer to God."

She was throwing missiles again. Haala was not giving up. It was as though she was a woman on a serious mission. Adamma was defending herself with the word of God. Every convincing act or powerful speech Haala made that caused Adamma to shake; Adamma will go back to the scriptures and renewed her strength. The enemy was causing her great uncertainty, but the word of God was the only weapon that was helping her to stand and not join forces with the opposite side because they were such a convincing, powerful and manipulative group.

From deep within her heart Adamma knows that great watchfulness will be needed. There is to be among God's people no spiritual stupidity. Evil spirits are actively engaged in seeking to control the minds of human beings. Men are binding up in bundles, ready to be consumed by the fires of the last days. Those who discard Christ and his righteousness will accept the sophistry that is flooding the world. Christians are to be sober and vigilant steadfastly resisting their adversary the Devil, who is going about as a roaring lion, seeking whom he may devour. Satan works through agents. He selects those who have not been drinking of the living waters, whose souls are athirst for something new and strange and who are ever ready to drink at any fountain that presents itself. (Ellen G. White Selected Messages, book 2, p. 53)

CHAPTER 34

As she sat in the church, awaiting the other members, Adamma could hear Sister Haala speaking to Brother Title in an upset manner.

"Some people are saying that I am worshipping the Devil, but I know God is answering my pray. If I am worshipping the Devil, why is God still answering my pray? I even told God, God if you know that I am not

doing the right thing, stop answering my pray. I love the Lord and I love him genuinely and when I go to God, I go to him honestly! I was even telling Brother Thomas, if nobody wants Jesus I will take him all for myself. I have grown to love God so much it is just amazing and nothing is going to prevent me from serving my God!"

As soon as the church business meeting was over, Adamma walked behind Sister Haala and Sister Novella. She could hear their conversation as they awaited a bus.

"Haala, Sister Cairoshell is so nice sometimes she just makes my day. She has any children?"

"Yes, yes a big son and…..…"

Adamma took a bus and went home. Adamma realized that some church members were finding themselves into a dangerous trap. As she walked up the steps to her home, Adamma knew in her heart that God cannot be mocked. She reflected on her once close friend, who appeared to be strong, well grounded, pompous and firmly set in her ways to destruction. Adamma reflected on 2 Timothy 4:3- 4: *'For the time will come when men will not put up with sound doctrine. Instead, to suit their own desires, they will gather around them a great number of teachers to say what their itching ears want to hear. And they shall turn away their ears from the truth, and shall be turned unto fables.'*

It was Sister Haala's turn to do the lesson study. She stood in front the class.

"Today our lesson study is captioned Jesus and the social outcasts. First I must raise the question who is a social outcast? Let us hear Brother Johnny," she remarked.

"A social outcast is anyone society deems as unimportant."

"I quite agree on that. Thanks Brother Johnny for your input. Sometimes there are people who are in bad shape whether mentally, spiritually or physically and for whatever reason, we have to view them in the way that we think our unconditionally loving God views them. Let us hear Sister Onika." She pointed to the woman.

"As children of God we have to realize that we are all equal in his sight. We cannot be behaving as though some persons are more important than others. We have to treat each other with love and don't discriminate."

"Thanks sister. Yes, we have to realize at the end of the day, we all need love and affection and we cannot go about isolating ourselves from people because we are all God's children."

Adamma could see a slight smile on Haala's face.

Adamma stared Haala intently in her face. *You really tell yourself I am joking with you.* Feeling angry of what she was encountering, Adamma reminded herself that God's holy words must come to pass. Sitting quietly in her anger, she meditated on 1 Timothy chapter 4 1:2: *'Now the spirit speaketh expressly, that in the later times some shall depart from the faith, giving heed to seducing spirits and doctrines of devils. Speaking lies in hypocrisy; having their conscience seared with a hot iron.'*

CHAPTER 35

It was December 1995, on a cold, windy night, when Adamma Guidance, climbed the steep hill to the Higher Calling Church. They were having a communion service. As she entered the church, she quietly took a seat.

One hour later, as the members went to the back of the church to do the foot washing and the deaconesses and deacons get ready to line up to enter into the church, Sister McCord opened her hands in a gesture of concern. Adamma knew the older woman meant it was a long time I haven't seen you. Adamma playfully clapped the woman's open hands.

From the back row she could see Sister Reign adjusting her glasses while looking at her.

God, please calm this woman for me. Lord you already know my grave situation.

"Sister Adamma you at church, I didn't even know you were here."

"Yes, I am right here."

She could see a few others focusing their attention on her.

The sound of the pianist chord signaled the deaconesses and deacons to walk into the church; Adamma Guidance breathed a sigh of relief as she walked along with the others.

As the service ended, Brother Harvard reminded the members to continue to prayer for Sister Rebecca who was hospitalized. On hearing the announcement, Adamma decided to visit her soon.

She lingered a few minutes to greet her other brothers and sisters in Christ then took a bus and went home.

A few days later, as she walked along the narrow hallway toward the female surgical ward, Adamma could smell the antibiotics. It was a scent she had grown accustomed too while visiting the hospital over the years. On entering the female surgical ward at a far corner to her right, she spotted Sister Rebecca lying on her back on a narrow, white bed. As she approached her, the ill woman offered a warm smile while weakly raising her left hand. As she stood by her sister in faith bedside, Adamma gave her words of encouragement to build her hope. Twenty minutes later, Adamma spotted Sister Haala heading towards Sister Rebecca. She was dressed all in white with two women accompanying her. As they arrived at Sister Rebecca's bedside, she greeted them wholeheartedly. They too were offering great words of encouragement. Moments later, Sister Rebecca turned to Sister Haala and directed a question at her.

"So you come to do your prayer as usual, what days you come again at the hospital?"

At the question, Adamma stared Haala in her face. Haala slightly turned her face away.

"Mondays and Wednesdays."

"In times like this, we all do need praying for. This is such a wonderful ministry you all have going, may God continue to bless you all."

The sick woman gentle squeezed Haala's hand.

Not having the courage to be around them, Sister Adamma said a teary goodbye to Sister Rebecca. On leaving, she saw Haala putting her right hand on Sister Rebecca's shoulder to offer a word of prayer. As Adamma walked out the room, she was deeply troubled. Jeremiah chapter 12: verse 5 came to memory which offered words of encouragement to her soul.

If thou hast run with the footmen, and they have wearied thee, then how canst thou contend with horses? And if in the land of peace, wherein thou trustedst, they wearied thee, then how wilt thou do in the swelling of Jordan?

Adamma knows Satan is putting forth his utmost efforts for a final struggle against Christ and his followers. Antichrists are performing their marvelous works in the presence of men. The counterfeits resemble the truth that it is almost impossible to distinguish between them except by the Holy Scriptures. By their testimony every statement and every miracle must be tested! (Ellen .G. White The Great Controversy, p.593.)

Mrs. Adamma Guidance knows she will be up to a serious challenge and the powers of darkness will be extremely angry at her for exposing them. She knows they are a mighty force to reckon with, but Adamma

Guidance knows in her heart someone has to be bold and stand firm for the Lord. She knew that she either stood for God or compromised his holy words by choosing to be silent and let evil saturate the land.

Lord, it felt as though the sharp sword of the enemy almost destroyed me. God I have felt its deep penetration. Lord, it is as though I have barely made it, by a very thin, thread. Lord, you have allowed them to take me to the edge and just when I thought I was going to be done with, you have stepped in to up hold me.

God, I am not afraid to stand for you. I will stand God. I will stand and thank you Jehovah for allowing me to go through such immense pressure. Lord, if I had not suffered, I would have never known what was taking place, but the excruciating pain caused me to pay close attention of what was taking place around me. Lord, even in my darkest hours, I can trust you.

Adamma Guidance reflected strongly on *Ezekiel chapter 33: verse 6. But if the watchman see the sword come, and blow not the trumpet, and the people be not warned; if the sword come, and take any person from among them, he is taken away in his iniquity; but his blood will I require at the watchman's hand.*

She then listened to her heart. You cannot correct what you are unwilling to confront. Behaviour permitted is behaviour perpetuated to be continued. Who you really are, depends on what you do. You dare not compromised the word of God! Sometimes you have to take the bull by its horn and deal with it face on. It is impossible for you to lose with God. Impossible!

God determines what our location will be, at what time and place, for how long, what qualifications and training are necessary so that we can fit the task he has ordained for us.

EPILOGUE

Mrs. Adamma Guidance continued to read the words of the Bible on a daily basis and cement herself in the scriptures. The words are her only shield from Satan's demonic power. Adamma read the words and meditated.

1 John 4

Beloved, believe not every spirit, but <u>try the spirits whether they are of God:</u> because many false prophets are gone out into the world.

1 Timothy chapter 4 1:2

Now the spirit speaketh expressly, that in the latter times <u>some shall depart from the faith, giving heed to seducing spirits and doctrines of devils.</u> Speaking lies in hypocrisy; having their conscience seared with a hot iron.

As she finished reading, she thought of the church members who were attending the prayer meeting.

Acts chapter 20: 29-31

For I know this, that after my departing shall <u>grievous</u> <u>wolves enter in among you, not sparing the flock. Also</u> <u>of your ownselves shall men arise, speaking perverse</u> <u>things, to draw away disciples after them.</u> Therefore watch, and remember, that by the space of three years I ceased not to warn everyone night and day with tears.

Isaiah chapter 30 verse 13

Therefore this iniquity shall be to you as a breach ready to fall, swelling out in a high wall, whose breaking cometh suddenly at an instant.

Jeremiah chapter 6 verse 15

Were they ashamed when they had committed abomination? Nay, they were not at all ashamed, neither could they blush: therefore they shall fall among them that fall: at the time that I visit them they shall be cast down, saith the Lord.

Jeremiah chapter 5 verse 31

The prophets prophesy falsely, and the priests bear rule by their means; and my people love to have it so: and what will ye do in the end thereof?

Deuteronomy chapter 13 verses 1-4

If there arise among you a prophet, or a dreamer of dreams, and giveth thee a sign or a wonder, And the sign or the wonder come to pass, whereof he spake unto thee, saying, let us go after other gods, which thou hast not known, and let us serve them; Thou shalt not hearken unto the words of that prophet, or that dreamer of dreams: for the Lord your God proveth you, to know whether ye love the Lord your God with all your heart and with all your soul.

Ezekiel chapter 22 verse 25

There is a conspiracy of her prophets in the midst thereof, like a roaring lion ravening the prey; they have devoured souls; they have taken the treasure and precious things; they have made her many widows in the midst thereof.

2 Peter chapter 2 verses 2-3

And many shall follow their pernicious ways; by reason of whom the way of truth shall be evil spoken of. And through covetousness shall they with feigned words make merchandise of you: whose judgment now of a long time lingereth not, and their damnation slumbereth not.

Titus 1 chapter 10-11

For there are many <u>unruly</u> and <u>vain talkers</u> and <u>deceivers</u> specially they of the circumcision: <u>whose mouths must be stopped, who subvert whole houses, teaching things which they ought not, for filthy lucre's sake.</u>

Her mind recalled all the evil things Afafa, Gada and Sister Cairoshell were saying that the Holy Spirit revealed to them.

Revelation chapter 16 verses 13 and 14

And I saw three unclean spirits like frogs come out of the mouth of the dragon, and out of the mouth of the beast, and out of the mouth of the false prophet. <u>For they are the spirit of devils, working miracles, which go forth unto the kings of the earth and of the whole world, to gather them to the battle of that great day of God almighty.</u>

2 Corinthians 11:13-15

For such are false prophets, deceitful workers, <u>transforming themselves into the apostles of Christ. And no marvel; for Satan himself is transformed into an angel of light. Therefore it is no great thing if his ministers also be transformed as the ministers of righteousness; whose end shall be according to their works.</u>

A loud alarm went off in Adamma's head, as she read that scripture, she thought about the white clothes Sister Cairoshell had her followers wearing. They were indeed being transformed into angels of light.

Jeremiah 23:30-32

Therefore, behold, I am against the prophets, saith the Lord, that steal my words from his neighbour. Behold, I am against the prophet saith the Lord, that use their tongues, and say, he saith. <u>Behold, I am against them that prophesy false dreams, saith the Lord, and do tell them, and cause my people to err by their lies, and by their lightness; yet I sent them not, nor commanded them: therefore they shall not profit these people at all, saith the Lord.</u>

Adamma reflected on the dreams Haala was telling her consistently and claiming with all her heart she got those dreams.

Matthew chapter 7 verses 21-23

Not everyone that saith unto me, Lord, Lord, shall enter into the Kingdom of heaven; but he that doeth the will of my father which is in heaven. <u>Many will say unto me in that day, Lord, Lord, have we not prophesied in thy name? And in thy name have cast out devils? and in my name done many wonderful works? And then I</u>

will profess unto them, I never knew you: depart from me, ye that work iniquity.

Romans chapter 16:17-18

Now I beseech you, brethren, mark them which cause divisions and offences contrary to the doctrine which ye have learned; and avoid them. For they that are such serve not our Lord Jesus Christ, but their own belly; and by good words and fair speeches deceive the hearts of the simple. (People who are naïve.)

1 Timothy chapter 6:10

For the love of money is the root of all evil: which while some coveted after, they have erred from the faith, and pierced themselves through with many sorrows.

Acts chapter 13 verses 6-12

And when they had gone through the isle unto Pa'phos, they found a certain sorcerer, a false prophet, a Jew, whose name was Bar-je'-sus: which was with the deputy of the country, Ser'-gi-us Pau-lus, a prudent man; who called for Bar-na-bas and Saul, and desired to hear the word of God. But El-y-mas the sorcerer (for so is his name by interpretation) withstood them, <u>seeking to turn away the deputy from the faith.</u> Then Saul, (who is also called Paul,) filled with the Holy Ghost, set his eyes on him, And said, o full of all subtilty and all mischief, thou child of the Devil, thou enemy of all righteousness, wilt thou not cease to pervert the right ways of the Lord? And now, behold, the hand of the Lord is upon thee, and thou shalt be blind, not seeing the sun for a season. And immediately there fell on him a mist and darkness: and he went about seeking some to lead him by the hand. Then the deputy, when he saw what was done, believed, being astonished at the doctrine of the Lord.

Adamma reflected on Haala claiming strongly that Sister Cairoshell is a true prophetess, but when Gada and Afafa entered her prayer meeting, she couldn't detect they were counterfeits instead she said whatever they have to say the Lord said she must allowed them to say it. Instead they have joined forces. Can light and darkness walked hand in hand? What fellowship does light has with darkness? Is God the author of confusion?

Ephesians chapter 5 verses 10-12

Finally, my brethren, be strong in the Lord, and in the power of his might. <u>Put on the whole armour of God, that ye may be able to stand against the wiles of the Devil. For we wrestle not against flesh and blood, but against principalities, against powers, against the rulers of the darkness of this world, against spiritual wickedness in high places.</u>

Psalms 37 verse 38

But the transgressors shall be destroyed together: the end of the wicked shall be cut off.

Mark chapter 13 verse 37

And what I say unto you I say unto all, <u>watch.</u>

1 John chapter 1 verses 5-6

This then is the message which we have heard of him, and declare unto you, that <u>God is light, and in him is no</u>

darkness at all. If we say that we have fellowship with him, and walk in darkness, we lie, and do not the truth.

1 Kings chapter: 13

After reading that portion of scripture, (1Kings chapter: 13) Adamma knows within her heart she has to be obedient to God words and obey it directly. She thought about what the Bible says, when a prophet speaketh in the name of the Lord if the thing follow not nor come to pass, the prophet has spoken presumptuously. This particular scripture had taught her a valuable lesson. You must take the word of God for exactly what it is otherwise you are in serious trouble!

Jeremiah chapter 28 10-17

Then Hananiah the prophet took the yoke from off the prophet Jeremiah's neck, and break it. And Hananiah spake in the presence of all the people saying thus saith the Lord; Even so will I break the yoke of Nebuchadnezzar king of Babylon from the neck of all nations within the space of two full years. And the Prophet Jeremiah went his way. Then the word of the Lord came unto Jeremiah the prophet, after that Hananiah the prophet had broken the yoke from off the neck of the prophet Jeremiah saying, Go tell Hananiah, saying, thus saith the Lord; Thou hast broken the yokes of wood; but thou shalt make for them yokes of iron. For thus saith the Lord of hosts, the God of Israel I have put a yoke of iron upon the neck of all these nations, that they may serve Nebuchadnezzar king of Babylon; and they shall serve him: and I have given them the beast of the field also. Then saith the prophet Jeremiah unto Hananiah the prophet, hear now, Hananiah; the Lord hath not sent thee; but thou makest this people to trust in a lie. Therefore thus saith the Lord; Behold, I will cast thee from the face of the earth: this year thou shall die, because thou has taught rebellion against the Lord.

Ephesians chapter 5 verses 11-13

And have no fellowship with the unfruitful works of darkness, but rather reprove them. For it is shameful even to speak of those things which are done by them in secret, but all things that are reproved are made manifest by the light, for whatever makes manifest is light.

Nahum chapter 1 verse 9

What do you conspire against the Lord? He will make an utter end of it. <u>Affliction will not rise up a second time.</u>

Jeremiah chapter 23 verse 40

And I will bring an everlasting reproach upon you, and a perpetual shame, which will never be forgotten.

Adamma thought about Afafa in the pig pen with her buttocks exposed. The scriptures are indeed fulfilling.

Proverbs chapter 24 verse 8

He that deviseth to do evil shall be called a mischievous person.

Psalms 89 verses 20-23

I have found David my servant; with my holy oil have I anointed him: With whom my hand shall be established:

mine arm also shall strengthen him. The enemy shall not exact upon him; nor the son of wickedness afflict him. And I will beat down his foes before his face, and plague them that hate him.

Deuteronomy 20 verse 1

When you go out to battle against your enemies and see horses and chariots and people more numerous than you, do not be afraid of them for the Lord your God is with you.

After reading the text on a daily basis, Adamma's mind felt clear and ready to face the challenges of the day. It is indeed her only source of strength and courage to face life and its many shocking, unpredictable curves.

REFERENCES

Holy Bible King James version

White, Ellen (1972) True Revival The Church's Greatest Need.

WWW.Letusreason.org

Christian- talk.forumotion.com

Seventh- Day Adventist Hymnal word edition

The Methodist Hymn Book

SYNOPSIS

The Unmockable Master is a story of two young women, Adamma Guidance and Haala Snow whose main goal was to make it into God's eternal Kingdom. Both women had a dynamic prayer life and so, their friendship skyrocketed causing them to trust each other.

It all shattered when Haala's cousin, Afafa and her companion Gada entered their lives. They had appeared as angels of light. They revealed things that appeared true and did many wonderful works in the name of the Lord. Along with another sister in faith, Sister Cairoshell, they had a prayer meeting that caught the eyes of many believers in Christ. At these prayer meetings prophecies were made hooking and bundling many victims, as they became spell bound into a deadly trap of deceit. It was later discovered these people sought an ungodly source!

Sadly, some people continue with false ideologies and teachings, contrary to God's will. Consequently, the hurt and sufferings are manifesting itself in all corners of the Earth.

<u>Galatians 6 verse 7: Be not deceived; God is not mocked: for whatsoever a man soweth, that shall he also reap.</u>

Printed in the United States
By Bookmasters